UNDER THE OLD COVENANT:

BOOK 1: SACRIFICES AND OFFERINGS

BOOK 2: THE FESTIVALS OF JEHOVAH

BOOK 3: LESSONS FROM PRAYER

DR. A.T. DOODSON

Copyright © Hayes Press 2018

All rights reserved. No part of this book may be reproduced, stored in a retrieval system, or transmitted in any form, without the written permission of Hayes Press.

Published by:

HAYES PRESS Publisher, Resources & Media

The Barn, Flaxlands

Royal Wootton Bassett

Swindon, SN4 8DY

United Kingdom

www.hayespress.org

Unless otherwise indicated, all Scripture quotations are from the HOLY BIBLE, the Revised Version (Public Domain, 1885). Scriptures marked KJV are from the Holy Bible, King James Version (Public Domain, 1611).

TABLE OF CONTENTS

BOOK ONE – SACRIFICES AND OFFERINGS UNDER THE OLD COVENANT

1. INTRODUCTION

2. A SWEET SAVOUR

3. FORGIVENESS, ATONEMENT AND ACCEPTANCE

4. THE DISTINCTION BETWEEN SIN AND TRESPASS

5. THE COMPONENTS OF THE OFFERING

6. THE MEAL-OFFERING

7. THE DUTIES OF THE OFFEROR

8. THE DUTIES OF THE PRIESTS

9. THE WORK OF THE PRIEST

10. THE SPRINKLING, POURING AND SCATTERING OF THE BLOOD

11. THE FOOD OF THE PRIESTS

12. THE TITHE AND THE FREE-WILL OFFERINGS

BOOK TWO: THE FESTIVALS OF JEHOVAH UNDER THE OLD COVENANT

1. THE FESTIVALS

2. THE SABBATH

3. THE BEGINNING OF MONTHS

4. THE DAYS OF UNLEAVENED BREAD

5. THE SHEAF OF FIRSTFRUITS

6. THE FEAST OF WEEKS

7. THE GLEANING OF THE HARVEST

8. THE FEAST OF TRUMPETS

9. THE DAY OF ATONEMENT

10. THE FEAST OF TABERNACLES

11. THE YEAR OF JUBILEE (LEVITICUS 29)

BOOK THREE – LESSONS FROM PRAYER

1. SOME PRINCIPLES OF PRAYER

2. THE PRAYERS OF ABRAHAM

3. THE PRAYERS OF JACOB

4. THE PRAYERS OF MOSES

5. MOSES, A DISCOURAGED MAN OF GOD

6. THE DESPONDENCY OF JOSHUA

7. HANNAH AND SAMUEL

8. THE PRAYERS OF DAVID

9. THE PRAYERS OF SOLOMON

10. THE PRAYERS OF DANIEL, EZRA AND NEHEMIAH

11. THE PRAYER OF JONAH

BOOK ONE - SACRIFICES AND OFFERINGS UNDER THE OLD COVENANT

CHAPTER ONE: INTRODUCTION

The offerings which feature so prominently in the ordinances of the law provide a rich treasury for the student of the Scriptures, though their study is too frequently neglected because of the apparent complexity of the various ordinances. The truths of Leviticus are not generally found on the surface, and it is only the earnest student who delights unaided to dig for gems of truth to be found in that book. It is our purpose, therefore, to enlist the sympathy of fellow students in a survey of the offerings, as to their different objects, their relationships, the spiritual lessons to be derived, and, above all the glimpses they give of the Lord whose glorious Person and work are set forth by them.

The Epistle to the Hebrews gives sufficient warranty for not dismissing these teachings as "Jewish things," for it gives a vital connecting link between the ordinances of the Old Covenant and those of the New Covenant, and makes us realise that there is something more than the Passover to be considered by a redeemed people. For "even the first covenant had ordinances of divine service" (Hebrews 9:1), and the word even (or verily or indeed) emphasises the fact that it was an essential part of the covenant for service to be thus rendered, and that all these things must find a correspondence in the day of reformation, or setting right. There is, alas, too often a view expressed that the New Covenant has done away with the ordinances of the Old Covenant to such an extent that the glorious liberty of the disciple must not be marred by any seeking of knowledge as to the way of service.

Such as hold these views have little sympathy with a study of the types and shadows of the law, because these reveal that the principles of God are much the same in every age, and that the worshipper must be as careful today as any Israelite in a past day as to his service and as to his way of approach. It is necessary today to remember that the service which is well pleasing to God must be offered with as much reverence and awe as ever God enjoined at mount Sinai (Hebrews 12:18-29). We are indeed not come to such a mount where a holy God speaks through the tangible things of creation, but we are come to One whose conception of His own holiness and righteousness found expression in His own Son. If indeed we are not called upon to witness that clouds and darkness are round about Him, we are expected to know, and to appreciate to our utmost power, that righteousness and judgment form the foundation of His throne (Psalm 97:2).

Unless there is a deep apprehension of the attributes of God, there can be but little understanding of the possibilities of serving Him; if we do not attempt to understand what is proper to offer to God we are in greater ignorance than those who were under the law. It was never intended that the annulment of the law should lead to such misconceptions of the sacrifices well pleasing to God as are found in this so-called day of liberty. If a better Covenant is associated with a better Priest and a better Sacrifice than any to be found under the Old Covenant, it is surely to be expected that such better things would be accompanied by a better apprehension of the things of God than was possible to men of an earlier age.

The Book of Leviticus is indissolubly joined with the Book of Exodus, both being part of the Law of Moses, and the first word "And" shows that the subject matter is intimately related to the closing chapters of the Book of Exodus in which the Glorious Presence of God has been seen in association with His House. The Book of Leviticus opens by declaring that "Jehovah called unto Moses." Though God spoke much with Moses, the occasions when this expression is used are very noteworthy, whether at the Bush (Exodus 3:4), or at Sinai (Exodus 19:3 and 20) when the mountain quaked, or when he was called into the midst of the cloud for 40 days (Exodus 24:16), or, as in Leviticus, when God speaks from the place which He has chosen. The commands and the truths to be disclosed on these occasions are the weightiest of all, and on this occasion the purpose of God is to advise His people as to the mode of approach to Him now that He dwelt in their midst.

From the earliest days men had offered up burnt offerings and sacrifices, so that there is nothing essentially new about the offerings to be referred to, it is taken for granted that the people already know much about burnt offerings and peace offerings and so forth, but the people among whom God actually dwelt must be better instructed than their fathers, their apprehension of the claims of God must be deeper, their knowledge more detailed, their hearts more filled with reverence and awe now that God is so very near. Such must also be the object of our studies if we are to gain real benefit from them. It is the desire to please God which is a basis for sacrifice and offerings, and from the earliest times there have been men who sought a way of pleasing God. Cain and Abel both had this desire, but their apprehension of the truth and ways of God was not the same, so that Cain suffered the mortification of seeing his offering rejected.

God Himself pointed the moral, "If thou doest well, shalt thou not be accepted?" Noah offered a burnt-offering (Genesis 8:20), and his doing so calls for no comment in the context, so that it appears that from the very earliest times the essence of the teachings as to the offerings was known to men. It may be noted, however, that the offerings made prior to the erection of the Tabernacle appear to show very little discrimination as to the purpose and character of the offering, so that Jacob, for instance, in Genesis 31:54 and 46:1 offered "sacrifices," apparently of a general kind, while in Job 42:8 the offerings to be made on account of the folly of the friends of Job are specified as burnt-offerings. In fact the generalised conception of the value of an offering seems to have been with a view to showing God that the offerer was prepared to demonstrate his recognition of the fact that from the fall in Eden man could only be accepted through the shedding of the blood of a sacrificial victim.

However much or little men understood of the One who was to fulfil God's great purpose, this at least they did understand, that God had signified, to Abel and to Cain, and thence to all men, that this approach by sacrifice would secure the favour of God. In the fuller knowledge now to be revealed as God calls to Moses, there is to be a discrimination made, so that the offerer will be called upon to understand what it is he is about to do. No longer will it be considered according to knowledge to offer up a general sacrifice with a confused apprehension as to how much of it is for the acknowledgment of wrong-doing, or how much for propitiation or the securing of divine complacency. In this dispensation our sacrifices may be of a different nature, but there arise circumstances in which it is needful to know when the sacrifices of a broken heart (one that is conscious of sin) may be more appropriate than the sacrifices of thanksgiving, though many are but too ready to engage in the offering up of spiritual sacrifices in thanksgiving and praise when there is need for confession and reconciliation. The former things we should do, but the latter should not be left undone.

Any efforts which we make to understand the will of God and His truth will be regarded by Him as an acceptable sacrifice whether it be in the application of His word to personal shortcomings, or in those having to do with communion with Him, or in those which touch the appreciation of Himself and His attributes. All these things are to be found exemplified in the offerings of Leviticus, in the broad classes of the burnt-offering, the meal-offering, the peace-offering, the sin-offering and the trespass-offering, but even within each class of offering there are found different grades, and it is generally held that these refer to the different degrees of apprehension of the truths associated with the class of offering. All believers have not the same degree of apprehension of spiritual truth. There can be no doubt whatever that the offerings set forth different aspects of the Person and work of Christ, whether He is seen as One that died for our sins as the sin-offering, or as the One who has forever delighted the heart, of God by giving Himself as the burnt offering, or as the One who brings God and man together in the enjoyment of the peace-offering.

The most excellent way of studying the offerings is not that of taking the verses seriatim, but by arranging the details in parallel columns for the various offerings. It is not feasible to print such an arrangement, but its advantages will be gained by considering the contrasts and comparisons so revealed. This method, however, supposes that the student will have a measure of familiarity with the offerings, even if it be only through a simple perusal of the first few chapters of Leviticus. It will be then seen that there are five principal classes of offerings, which we shall arrange in two classes under the titles of

> (1) sweet savour offerings: the burnt-offering, the meal offering, and the peace-offering (Leviticus 1:9,13,17; 2:2, 9; 3:5,16);

> (2) forgiveness offerings: the sin-offering, and the trespass offering (Leviticus 4:20,26, 31,35; 5:10,13,16,18; 6:7).

We will begin our study with the sweet savour offerings.

CHAPTER TWO: A SWEET SAVOUR

It is a well-known principle of study that the first references to a word or subject in the Scriptures have a special bearing upon the interpretation and application, and the principle is exemplified in this instance also. For the first reference to a sweet savour offering is found in Genesis 8:20-22, where Noah offers of every clean beast and of every clean fowl a burnt-offering to the LORD: "And the LORD smelled the sweet savour; and the LORD said in His heart, I will not again curse the ground any more for man's sake. " Now the word for "sweet" is the Hebrew word 'niychoach' — "pleasant," and it is derived from another word 'nuwach' - "to rest or to settle down." It is a matter of very great interest and importance to notice that another derivative of this same word is Noach = nowach = "quiet or rest" and that this word is the name Noah.

Thus at the very outset of our studies we are caused to consider the bearing of the offerings on the important matter of rest. When this subject of rest is brought before us in the Scriptures we always have a connection with the eternal rest which will be enjoyed in Heaven, which God has visualised for Himself and the redeemed from times eternal, which has been set forth for enjoyment in time in connection with the Sabbath, the land of promise, the House of God in that land, and the House of God in the present day. That eternal rest will have its duties and privileges even as the rest of the believers has in this day. The two things are linked together, though at times it is necessary to distinguish between the eternal rest, and the present rest, which is for "Today" (see Hebrews 4).

When Noah offered burnt-offerings it was with some understanding of the peace and rest which he enjoyed and which was also pleasant to the LORD. It was his first duty in those scenes which were to him the equivalent to a new creation, and in the day when God will indeed make all things new it will be our duty and our privilege to enter into the appreciation of the rest of God, but it will be in connection with a better sacrifice, even our Lord Jesus Christ, that we shall render the offerings of our lips as an offering pleasant indeed to God. It is the privilege of a new creation in Christ Jesus to anticipate that day and also to enjoy, in measure, that rest in its present-day aspect.

The principal characteristics of the burnt-offering are denoted by the Hebrew and Greek words used to describe it, the former being holah = "that which ascends," and the latter being holocaust = "a whole burnt-offering". Practically speaking, the whole of the animal was offered to God, was wholly consumed, and ascended unto God in the sweet-smell. The offerer received nothing, all was for the enjoyment of the LORD. When Noah so offered his burnt-offerings it was with a single-minded desire to express unto his God his appreciation of the goodness and excellencies of the One whose awful powers had been made manifest in the upheaval of the great deep, and in the dreadful doom of the wicked men with whom the Spirit of God had striven in vain, while at the same time there was recognition of the grace and saving power of Him who had caused Noah to build an ark for the saving of his house.

When Noah saw the ascending smoke he saw therein an outward and visible sign of an inward and spiritual grace, he saw a symbol of that which his thankful heart could feel but could never express, and with spiritual insight and instructed knowledge he approached his great God and Saviour by offering the token of a devoted life. We thus see that to Noah there was implied by the burnt-offering many things which were associated with thanksgiving and praise. The burnt-offering was a full offering, and it will be well if we also understand from the outset that from of old the burnt-offering implied all that could be expressed, though men might never utter a word. It would be very wrong to think that the various types of offerings were mutually exclusive (though, as was pointed out in the previous chapter, the different offerings were designed to increase the spiritual discernment), and in fact we shall see that in some of the grades of the offerings there is a merging of thought with that normally expressed by another type of offering.

In a similar way, while the meal-offering appears to be entirely different from the burnt-offering, in that no life was offered, and it was not all for God, yet the expression frequently occurs, "burnt-offering and its meal-offering." In Numbers 15:8-9 it is laid down that when a burnt-offering was presented before God it must be accompanied by a meal-offering. Also a peace-offering is so like a burnt-offering, both as regards the animals offered, and the grades of the offerings, that the comparison calls aloud for attention, and we see that the principal difference is that it is not wholly an ascending offering, but that in addition to a part being devoted to God and to the priests, as in the meal-offering (God alone having a portion in the burnt-offering), the offerer, his family, and even his friends, have portions of the peace-offering. We see something of this in connection with Noah. Primarily, his offering was wholly for God, and he offered it unconditionally, but this, while exceedingly precious to the heart of God, would not content the God of grace who longs for His creatures to share in the joy and blessing, so that we read the response of God as to the ground, and the blessing to the creatures, while to Noah He gives a portion also.

"And God blessed Noah ... and said ... Every moving thing that liveth shall be food for you ... And I will establish My covenant with you ..." It needs very little exposition of this to show that in this act of grace we get something of the peace-offering prefigured, in which there is a wide-spread sharing and communion. The burnt-offering so aptly expresses the unreserved devotion of the Lord Jesus that one is tempted to linger and to muse upon Him of whom it speaks. "Christ ... gave Himself up for us, an offering and a sacrifice to God, for an odour of a sweet smell" (Ephesians 5:2). There is not here any suggestion of His giving Himself for the sin of the world, such as we get elsewhere, for the words "an odour of a sweet smell" preclude the thought. It requires no great stretch of the imagination to read the context in the light of the dealings of God with Noah.

From verse 25 of Ephesians 4 we have a list of things which might well take our thoughts back to the days when God saw that the wickedness of man was very great in the earth (compare Genesis 6:1-8 with Ephesians 4:25-32). when the LORD said, "My Spirit shall not strive with man for ever." The Apostle passes from the contemplation of such a state of affairs in his hearers as he exhorts that the Spirit be not grieved, and contemplates the new creation in Christ Jesus, saying, "Walk in love, even as Christ also loved you and gave Himself for you." Just as Noah's offering up of an odour of a sweet smell was a delightful and perhaps necessary preliminary to a proper walk in that new scene, with judgment accomplished, so also is Christ's offering up of Himself in all His fragrance accepted of God that we might walk before Him in new creation life. This thought is strengthened by what we read in Hebrews 5:7 concerning the value of the life of the Lord Jesus, for His life and His death are joined together in the counsel of God for us. His unreserved offering up of Himself is the anti-type of the burnt-offering while the anti-type of the meal-offering is seen in His life, and we have already noticed that the meal-offering was an adjunct to the burnt-offering.

The meal-offering was also a sweet savour offering and the perfect life of the Lord Jesus is vital in connection with His appearing for us before God, named of God a high priest after the order of Melchizedek. Without this sweet savour offering to God it would be hopeless for us to know the power of walking in new creation life. It is with reverence and awe that we are also constrained to note the profound words of the Apostle Paul in 2 Corinthians 2:15: "For we are a sweet savour of Christ unto God." When Jacob sought a blessing from his earthly father he sought it in the garb of another, and so obtained the blessing, as Isaac exclaimed. "See, the smell of my son is as the smell of a field which the LORD hath blessed" (Genesis 27:27; see also Hosea 14:6). But we, without guile, receive a blessing as the sweet savour of another ascends unto God through and in us.

While the sweet savour offerings primarily speak of Christ it is permitted unto us to offer on our own account, through the grace of Christ in us, as we see from Philippians 4:18. Paul speaks of the things received from the Philippian saints as "an odour of a sweet smell, a sacrifice acceptable, well-pleasing unto God" and we note how that the peace-offering is suggested in the next verse, as the Apostle says, "And my God shall fulfil every need of yours according to His riches in glory in Christ Jesus."

CHAPTER THREE: FORGIVENESS, ATONEMENT, AND ACCEPTANCE

The preciousness of the sweet savour offerings, both to God and men, is that they are associated with communion in various aspects. Beyond all doubt, when man was created in the image of God, when life was breathed into His nostrils, it was to this intent, that in the fulness of life he might know his Creator, and that he might in some measure share in the fellowship which already existed between the Persons of the Trinity. The greatest calamity which befell men when sin entered into the world was not so much the fact of death, but the loss of communion.

It was the realisation of this which filled up the cup of agony of the Lord Jesus, when He cried that bitter cry, "My God, My God, why hast Thou forsaken Me?" If Christ was to be truly man, it was needful that He should experience the worst of Adam's woes, and to know the dreadfulness of the penalty for sin which He was bearing for Adam's race, and when God looked upon Him as the Sinbearer upon the Cross He was constrained to break that communion which had been so precious to the Lord throughout His earthly sojourn. It is sad that in the day in which we live men are encouraged in the religious services of professing Christendom to imagine themselves as partaking of communion when they have never considered the barriers to that communion.

In the Levitical Law there could never be any misunderstanding as to this, and the offerer had to recognise the fact of sin, whether known and confessed in wrongful acts, or whether recognised as the state in which men are found by nature. Thus we find two types of offerings which are called the Sin-offering and the Trespass-offering. The broad distinction between these two classes is that in the latter there are definite acts which become known to the offerer, and which, as they involve loss to others, require restitution to be made, while in the former the acts are not so prominent as the sinful state of the offerer, as we shall see on a later occasion. Both types of offering, however, are characterised by their being offered for forgiveness. If Leviticus 4 and 5 are scrutinised this will be very apparent. In general, as we see from many Scriptures, sin-offerings and trespass-offerings were always offered first, after which the sweet savour offerings could be acceptably rendered. "If Thou, LORD, shouldest mark iniquities, O LORD, who shall stand? But there is forgiveness with Thee, That Thou mayest be feared" (Psalm 130:4-5).

Forgiveness of sins has never been regarded by God as an end in itself, though selfish men would appear to be content with a one-sided relation with God. Forgiveness has an end in view, as we shall seek to show, but we are constrained to consider for a little while the importance of forgiveness in the purposes of God. Forgiveness is a divine attribute, as we see from Exodus 34:7, when Jehovah declared Himself to Moses as a God full of compassion and gracious, but it is only granted to men on account of a divine offering. It is through Christ that we have forgiveness of our trespasses, according to the riches of the grace of God (Ephesians 1:7). and that grace was made to abound unto us in all wisdom and prudence (verse 8). This means that it was one of the deep things of God that forgiveness should be made dependent upon the excellent work of Christ and not upon any of the works of men.

Whether a man offered much or little as a sin-offering, whatever be his apprehension of that which was speaking of Christ, the fact remains that in the word of God he could read at the end of the instruction for each grade of offering, "and he shall be forgiven." Forgiveness of our sins is never made to depend upon the degree of our apprehension of them nor upon the degree of our confession of them. We are forgiven because of the Beloved. It is instructive in this connection to consider the very first reference to forgiveness in the Scriptures. Please read Genesis 50:14-21:

> "And Joseph returned into Egypt, he, and his brethren, and all that went up with him to bury his father, after he had buried his father. And when Joseph's brethren saw that their father was dead, they said, "It may be that Joseph will hate us, and will fully requite us all the evil which we did unto him." And they sent a message unto Joseph, saying, "Thy father did command before he died, saying, 'So shall ye say unto Joseph, Forgive, I pray thee now, the transgression of thy brethren, and their sin, for that they did unto thee evil: and now, we

> pray thee, forgive the transgression of the servants of the God of thy father.'
>
> And Joseph wept when they spake unto him. And his brethren also went and fell down before his face; and they said, "Behold, we be thy servants." And Joseph said unto them, "Fear not: for am I in the place of God? And as for you, ye meant evil against me; but God meant it for good, to bring to pass, as it is this day, to save much people alive. Now therefore fear ye not: I will nourish you, and your little ones." And he comforted them, and spake kindly unto them."

The wisdom of Israel is made manifest, and that of his sons also, when the message is sent to Joseph, "Forgive ... the transgression of thy brethren, and their sin, ... and ... forgive the transgression of the servants of the God of thy father." After all that Joseph had experienced of them this must have indeed touched his heart, and he wept, saying, "Fear not: for am I in the place of God?" It was indeed wise that the plea for forgiveness should rise from the merely human one of "thy brethren" to that of "the servants of the God of thy father." That is the plane on which God Himself dispenses forgiveness. We would that this were more clearly realised by beloved fellow-saints.

The beloved apostle Paul teaches us again and again this truth that forgiveness is in Christ, whether the forgiveness of our sins which we did aforetime, or the forgiveness which we ourselves should exercise. The device of Satan would be to make forgiveness depend upon works (see 2 Corinthians 2:10-11), but when Paul forgave, it was in the person of Christ. Again he says, in Ephesians 4:32 and elsewhere, "Be ye kind ... forgiving each other, even as God also in Christ forgave you." If we were more ready to appreciate the joy attached to the forgiveness of our sins we should be the more ready to forgive the sins against us of the brother for whom Christ died.

"But some have no knowledge of God: I speak this to move you to shame." If we made our forgiveness to depend upon Christ, and not upon the degree of confession or restitution by the wrongdoer, we should be more conscious of the fruits of the Spirit within us. But some may say, What has the mutual forgiveness of saints to do with the offerings? Much in every way. "Forgive us our trespasses as we forgive those that trespass against us." The work of Christ in the offerings goes beyond the Cross, and no offering was ever accepted from an offerer unless the conditions were fulfilled. If the different grades of offerings represent different degrees of apprehension of Christ, the above Scripture teaches us that it is mere affrontery to ask for our trespasses to be forgiven "in His Name" when our acts show that we have so little apprehension or appreciation of Christ, as to refuse to forgive the trespass of the brother for whom Christ died.

In association with forgiveness the offerer was promised atonement, the expression which is used being, "the priest shall make atonement for him as concerning his sin, and he shall be forgiven." Strictly speaking, therefore, we should have considered the atonement before the forgiveness, but we desired to compare the atonement resulting from the offering for sin with the atonement referred to in connection with the burnt-offering. See Leviticus 1:4, where we read that when the offerer lays his hand upon the head of the burnt-offering "it shall be accepted for him to make atonement for him." This is the only reference to atonement in connection with the sweet-savour offerings, but for practically every grade of the sin-offerings and trespass-offerings the expression quoted above is repeated at the end of the instructions concerning each grade of offering. The atonement is seen first of all in connection with the burnt-offering and last of all in connection with the sin-offering.

There is thus a suggestion of a distinction between the uses of the word "atonement." The word 'kaphar' so translated in each case simply refers to a covering and it finds many applications in that sense. It is first used, and significantly so, of the ark, when Noah was commanded to pitch it within and without with pitch. (This is not the covering referred to in Genesis 8:14, for that covering was a cover of boards.) The pitch gave perfect protection from the deluge. The same word has a close derivative which is applied to a village on account of its protecting walls, and another derivative refers to the cover of the Ark, the Mercy Seat.

Thus, when the word is used in connection with the burnt-offering, it does not imply that there is any association with sin. The covering up of sin is the result of an offering for sin, in the sense of Daniel 9:42, "make reconciliation for iniquity," or "cover up iniquity." Such sins are then forgotten and the sinner comes not into judgment, but in the case of the burnt-offering the cover is granted as soon as the offerer identifies himself with the offering by laying his hand upon it. It is a cover of righteousness in which a man can draw near to a holy God. It is associated in thought with the garments of righteousness which will cover the redeemed in glory, a covering which is effective to the redeemed at all times as they draw near. So clearly are these two aspects of atonement differentiated in the Scriptures that for the burnt-offering we get the expression "accepted ... for atonement" and for the sin-offering we get " atonement for sin ... and he shall be forgiven."

The thought of acceptance is peculiar to the burnt offering and to the peace-offering (see Leviticus 7:18), and probably to all the sweet savour offerings. The word used is sometimes translated "well-pleasing." These conclusions are summarised by Paul in Philippians 4:18. where he refers to the gift which was as an odour of a sweet smell, a sacrifice acceptable, well-pleasing to God. The sin-offering was not for acceptance, for God never had delight in offerings for sin. It was a dreadful necessity that such offerings had to be made at all, but God was pleased to grant a cover for our sins and forgiveness for our iniquity that He might be feared with a godly fear, and that we might know the greater joy of the cover which gives us liberty to draw near in the sacrifice of praise.

CHAPTER FOUR: THE DISTINCTION BETWEEN SIN AND TRESPASS

Before proceeding to the consideration of the details of the offerings it is advantageous to consider the way in which the sin-offerings are sub-divided in chapters 4 and 5 of Leviticus, and also to consider the relations between these and the trespass-offerings. This analysis is more necessary for the forgiveness offerings than it is for the sweet-savour offerings, for the latter have well-marked characteristics, whereas there is a gradation between the sins of ignorance of Leviticus 4 and the more venial sins of trespass of Leviticus 6. It is not surprising, therefore, to find that there are certain sins, not involving loss to others, which are described in chapter 5, and for which a "guilt-offering" had to be offered, while a "guilt-offering" had also to be offered for trespass.

The apostle said, "I had not known sin, except through the law" (Romans 7:7), but sin in the sight of God has ever been present in the flesh. Sin is inherent in us, and we are oft-times ignorant of its working. "For I know that in me, that is, in my flesh, dwelleth no good thing, for to will is present with me, but to do that which is good is not" (Romans 7:18). However willing, however learned, a man may be in the things of God, he fails. It is for unwitting sin that Leviticus 4 provides, sin done in ignorance, but which cannot be excused on the ground of ignorance. When it became known (verses 14 and 23) it was necessary to bring an offering. In Leviticus 5:1-13, guilt is imputed and a guilt-offering had to be offered, but before this could be done it was necessary to make confession (verse 5), whereas confession is not explicitly demanded in chapter 4. The guilt-offering for such confessionary sins is not identical with the guilt-offering where trespass has been committed, as we shall see in a later occasion.

The two are associated, however, in thought, as both the confessionary sins and the trespasses arise from negligence or carelessness as to the claims of God and the claims of men. The Hebrew word for "sin" (chata) primarily means "to miss the mark," as an archer, or "to miss the way" or "make a false step," as in Proverbs 19:2 and Proverbs 8:36, whereas the word for guilt or trespass (asham) primarily has the idea of "negligence, especially in going or gait." A trespass arises from a failure in duty, while sin may be the error of a well-meaning man. As we said above, there are all possible gradations between the unwitting sins and the culpable sins of trespass. Where a trespass was committed it involved loss which had to be made good. Thus in Leviticus 5:15 and 17 the trespass might even be unwitting, but nevertheless the LORD had been deprived of that which was His due, whether in the "holy things of the LORD" (verse 15) or in "any of the things which the LORD hath commanded not to be done."

Such a loss was to be estimated by the priest in the coinage of the sanctuary (verses 15 and 18), and the characteristic of the trespass-offering is that not only must full restitution be made, but in addition a fifth-part had to be added (verse 16). A similar injunction is given concerning the misdemeanours against men (6:1-7). In the former cases the priest acts as recipient for the LORD and in the latter case the aggrieved person receives restitution and the added compensation. The trespass-offering is naturally, in many ways, the easiest to understand, for something apparent is involved, a sense of loss is felt, and the ideas of restitution and compensation are of a simple character. The sin of Adam was not so much sin in the sense of missing the mark as sin in the sense of trespass. Both are implied, of course, but the sin of Adam caused tremendous losses, not only to God, but also to men. This is beautifully brought out in Romans 5, which is perhaps the best commentary on the trespass-offering.

The apostle shows the trespass (verse 15) was that death had been brought into the world or "reigned from Adam until Moses, even over them that had not sinned after the likeness of Adam's transgression" (verse 14). It does not necessarily mean that there were people who had not so sinned, but the argument is that if there had been such people they would have suffered death through the transgression of another. The transgression of Adam was thus not only against God, but against all his descendants, and it could only be met by Adam or by that One who stood in Adam's place or undertook to pay Adam's indebtedness both to God and to man. He restored that which He took not away. So we read that the free gift received through Christ (verse 15) exceeded by "much more" the original trespass of Adam. And not only so, but in that those who followed Adam transgressed also in their day, all these trespasses were taken into account so that no man in the great day of judgment could make complaint that his dire plight was due to the faults or transgressions of his ancestors, thus "many trespasses" were taken into account in the "free gift" (verse 16).

So also in verse 20 the effect of the law is to involve much trespass, but all these were met by the Redeemer who stood in Adam's place. In the judgment, all who have not accepted Christ as standing to pay Adam's debts will have no room for complaint; they will not be able to justify themselves on the ground of hereditary sin, for there is One ready to pay all, yes and more than all. The trespass-offering not only envisages restitution, but compensation also, and the fifth part is brought out very beautifully in the words "much more" of verse 15, and again in verse 17, and again in verse 20; truly "grace did abound more exceedingly." The true "restitution" set against the reign of death is the reign of life in Christ Jesus (verse 17), with the added compensation that those who benefit by this trespass-offering are placed in a far better position than Adam ever enjoyed.

Theirs is a far better lot, to be placed, not in a garden which God made, but before Him in His holy place in exceeding joy. Blessed be the fifth-part and Him who pays it! But God also was transgressed against, and the Lord Jesus has met every claim that God could have had on Adam or his descendants. The joy or communion in or with His creatures was one of the losses sustained by God, His rest was broken, His glory unexpressed by men. But the One who undertook the debt had the joy of restoring communion, and He wrought a rest for God, and made man fit to exercise his true glory in using his mouth to the glory of God. The song of praise which the redeemed can sing was beyond the comprehension of Adam in Eden, as well as the angels, for they never knew, as we know, Christ as Redeemer. The communion we have is a better and more continuous communion than that enjoyed by Adam, the rest we have is a better rest, and we shall rise to heights of praise or adoration that Adam could not have attained to. However little the redeemed may understand it, God, is satisfied and more than satisfied with the fruits of Christ's work in standing for Adam's transgression. Hence, in the day of judgment, both God and men will have perfect satisfaction, and that day will see the trespass-offering fulfilled in all perfection.

CHAPTER FIVE: THE COMPONENTS OF THE OFFERINGS

The instructions concerning the animals or substances which might be brought, or which had to be brought, are so precise that it becomes us to try to ascertain the teaching concerning them. For this purpose the following summary will be useful:

- The Burnt-offering: (1) a male of the herd; or (2) a male of the flock; or (3) turtledoves or young pigeons.
- The Meal-offering: (1) fine flour, baked or unbaked; with (2) oil and frankincense and salt.
- The Peace-offering: (1) a male or female of the herd; or (2) a male or female of the flock.
- The Sin-offering: (1) a young bullock for the priest or the congregation; (2) a male goat for a ruler; (3) a female goat or a lamb for one of the people.
- The Guilt-offering: (1) a female lamb or goat; or (2) turtledoves or young pigeons; or (3) fine flour without oil and frankincense.
- The Trespass-offering: (1) a ram.

We see at once that there is a very definite order in the lists of offerings, which is given precisely as in Leviticus 1 to 6, and the significance to be attached to the various grades is brought out at once in connection with the sin-offering. It is clear that the sin of a priest or of the whole congregation is more grievous than that of a ruler, and this again is more grievous than that of one of the people. Hence a bullock has to be offered in the first case, as being intrinsically more valuable and also, as we shall see later, as having some typical teaching. Also we see that whereas in general the flock may be either of sheep or of goats, the distinction between the sins of a ruler and a common man are emphasised by offering a male goat in the former case and a female goat or lamb in the latter, from which law we deduce that the offering of a female animal must be regarded as inferior to that of a male.

From this we deduce (if we need to!) that the burnt-offering must be regarded as on a higher level than the peace-offering, in that the former specifies male offerings only, while the peace-offering could be a male or a female. We also see that the guilt-offering is on a lower plane than the sin-offering, showing that culpable sins which arise from negligence are not so grievous as unwitting sins which arise out of our very nature. This is so contrary to the general notions of men that it is worth emphasising. The natural man is so prone to look at the things made evident to his senses that he underestimates the unseen sinful nature, whereas God is ever more concerned with what we are than with what we have done. Again, man is so egotistical that the peace-offering, in which he has a share, might easily be regarded as more precious than the burnt-offering. It will be noted that an element of choice is allowed the offerer in all cases except the sin-offering and the trespass-offering.

In the former a distinction is made as to the status of the sinner, but in the latter all are on the same plane, and a ram must be offered by men of all degree. We pointed out in the last chapter that a trespass required this special guilt-offering, and on comparing the guilt-offerings we see that while the general guilt-offering (for the confessionary sins) was a female, this special guilt-offering (for trespass) had to be a male. From the preceding conclusions, we see therefore that trespass was regarded more seriously than the sins of negligence, in that the offering was of a higher character. Since it is the special cases which give most help in the elucidation of the details, we can further consider the trespass-offering with regard to the character of the animal specified in the law. The Hebrew word for a "ram" is the word 'ayil', which means "strength," and it is applied to many things which suggest strength, such as "mighty man, lintel, oak, post, tree."

This suggests that the principle of making the punishment fit the crime finds application here! For many trespasses come from misapplied strength, where the stronger preys on the weaker. We get a side-light on this from the words translated "lamb" and "he-lamb"; the former is 'sey', probably from the idea of pushing out to graze, while the latter is 'kebes', from a root meaning "to dominate," and it is applied to a male lamb just old enough to butt. Thus the ram is indeed an animal appropriate to trespass. Men rise against men, and nation against nation, and in Daniel's vision this is pictured by the pushing ram against which no beasts could stand (Daniel 8:4).

We get some very remarkable instruction from the meanings of the words translated "goat." There are two words so translated, the word 'ez', derived from a word meaning "stout," being used in connection with the burnt-offering and the peace-offering, while the word 'sair' is used of the goat to be offered up by a ruler for his unwitting sin. Naturally we conclude that some significance must be attached to the change of word, and on investigation we find that sair means "shaggy or rough" and the same word is translated "devils" in the KJV of Leviticus 17:7, which in the RV reads, "They shall no more sacrifice their sacrifices unto the he-goats, after whom they go a whoring."

This word comes from 'saar', a primitive root meaning "to storm," which is used of tempests and whirlwinds and of horrible fear (Jeremiah 2, 12 and Ezekiel 32:10). (Neither word is used for the goat referred to in Daniel 8). It is most interesting to observe that it is principally in connection with the sin-offering of the goats on the Day of Atonement (Leviticus 16) that the word sair is used. There can be no question that it is intended to convey that the sin-offering for the unwitting sin of a ruler and for the unwitting sin atoned for on the Day of Atonement is of a very fierce character, not only aggressive in the sullen manner of the ram, but aggressive and fierce withal. When we examine the words translated "bullock," we get very similar conclusions. Several words are used, but we need only mention two:

> (1) 'baqar', from a primitive root meaning " to turn over or plough," and generally translated "herd, oxen"; and
>
> (2) 'par' from a root meaning "to break up" in a violent sense, which is frequently translated "make of none effect," "frustrate."

In Leviticus 1:5 the burnt-offering ("bullock") is 'ben hab-baqar', "a son of the herd," and in Leviticus 4:3-4, the sin offering is 'par ben baqar', "bullock, son of the herd." The "son of the herd" refers mainly to a domestic animal, a tamed animal. We see something of its significance in Isaiah 11:7: "The lion shall eat straw like the ox." The word par is used in Psalm 22, the well-known Messianic Psalm:

"Many bulls [par] have compassed Me: Strong bulls [par] of Bashan have beset Me much. They gape upon Me with their mouths, As a ravening and a roaring lion." Thus undoubtedly when par is used there is a suggestion of fierceness and violence. It may be noted that while the Book of Leviticus consistently makes a distinction in the words used for a bullock for a burnt-offering or for a sin-offering, no distinction is made in the Book of Numbers, and in fact par is used frequently for burnt-offerings in Numbers 28 and 29.

The Book of Numbers gives a special view of many of the offerings, and Leviticus gives a purer typical teaching. We see, therefore, that in the Book of Leviticus as a general rule the principal offerings for sin and trespass are indicated by words which carry suggestions of aggressiveness and violence, whereas in the sweet-savour offerings the animals are described by words of a more placid character. The fierceness diminishes as we go down the scale of the sin-offerings, and in the guilt-offerings, which were for negligence, there is no such thought implied, either through the female sheep or harmless doves. This contrast in the character of the offerings is of some importance, and it is rather a pity that the translation of the words involved does not convey the full thoughts.

Some writers on the offerings have thus been led astray in their interpretation of the sin-offerings, through applying the details too freely in the Lord Jesus Christ. From what we have said about the bullock and the goat it would not be right to regard them as strictly typical of Him whose gentle character is seen in the lamb. It is very instructive to note that there is no provision in the law for a male lamb to be offered as a sin-offering, so that the Lamb of God which bears away the sin of the world is not expressly typified in any of the animals specified under the law. While we shall not be able to compare Him directly either to the bullock or to the goat, yet we shall be able to deduce certain principles finding exemplification in these offerings which can be applied to His perfect offering.

(It may be necessary to distinguish between what man saw in Christ and what God saw. What man saw may correspond to the rough exterior of the goat, and the unattractive shagginess of the Nazarite, the friend of publicans and sinners, herding with those whom the priests and Pharisees accounted unholy ones, no better than the satyrs or rough he-goats in their eyes. But what God saw was a life of perfectness, and a heart of purity and holiness in His blessed Son.)

While the sinner under the law was caused to identify himself with an animal suggesting the fierceness and lawlessness of sin, he could see in the burnt-offering fierceness subdued and strength brought into subjection to the needs of man and the service of God. There is thus a suggestion that men can only be regarded as a sweet savour when there is the same subjection. The bullock, "strong to labour" and giving "great increase" by his strength, is a fit animal for a burnt-offering to God, while in his untamed condition he is a picture of the effects of sin. The meal-offerings, of course, have quite different teaching in view, and they will be considered in the very next chapter.

CHAPTER SIX: THE MEAL-OFFERING

The meal-offering is so distinct from the other offerings as concerning its materials that we shall find it advantageous to discuss its general purport before considering the ingredients. Like the other sweet savour offerings, there is no thought of sin associated with it so that it speaks in an intimate way of the Lord Jesus Christ. Unlike the other offerings, life is not cut off or given up, but the fruit of the ground is offered to God. In a later chapter dealing with the food of the priests, we shall be concerned with the important fact that this offering was used for the sustenance of the priests after God had received His portion, whereas in the burnt-offering God receives practically all. We therefore see that this offering is in some way associated with the provision which the Lord has made for those who serve Him.

We must also bear in mind that the meal-offering was not offered alone, but was associated with the burnt-offering— "its meal offering" (Leviticus 23:13). The general significance of the meal-offering is most clearly brought out in Leviticus 23. To my mind, the instructions in that chapter concerning the Festivals of Jehovah reveal the purposes of God in a very characteristic way, whether it is by direct commandment or by omission of details given elsewhere. As I pointed out in another book "The Festivals of Jehovah", we must distinguish between the details of Leviticus 16 (which are for the Priest), the details of Numbers 28 and 29 (which are for the people), and the details of Leviticus 23 which give the essential elements from God's point of view. Now in connection with the Passover only a burnt-offering is specified, while in the next festival, that of the wave-sheaf, a burnt-offering had to be accompanied by a meal-offering and a drink-offering, and in the festival of weeks all classes of offerings are specified. The latter festival has to do with the reception by men of the work of the Lord on the Cross, so that a sin-offering is required, but it may be noted that there is a very unusual order of the offerings: burnt-offering, meal-offering, sin-offering, peace-offering.

The last, though it is a sweet-savour offering, is here seen after the sin-offering, for the peace-offering has to do with communion between men and God. It would appear, therefore, that there is a gradation of thought here which should help us. At the Cross, the work of Christ was a mystery to men, even to the disciples, but it was a delight to God. The resurrection of the Lord brings into view another aspect of His work, brought before us in the type of the first-fruits of the harvest, the sheaf of which was waved before God, a symbol of the fruits of abounding life. It is particularly to be noticed that the meal-offering is mentioned with considerable detail, so supporting the view that it is at the Resurrection of the Lord that the meal-offering begins to find its anti-type.

This suggestion that the meal-offering refers primarily to the resurrection life of the Lord Jesus may cause some surprise in the minds of those who are familiar with the interpretation of the meal-offering as referring to the earthly life of the Lord. It may be well to state that one of the great difficulties of interpretation of the offerings is to avoid mere conjecture, and the difficulty in the case of the meal-offering is greater than in the cases of the other offerings. We must endeavour to determine the principal purpose of each offering, and we must look to the guidance of the Scriptures for any direct connections which will help to give substance to the interpretation put forward. The ultimate purpose of God is what we have in mind when we say that the meal-offering finds its anti-type in the resurrection life of the Lord, which is a continual sweet savour to God, and this we shall now seek to show.

The relation between the meal-offering and the earthly life of the Lord Jesus will then be shown to follow naturally as we consider the ingredients, towards the end of this chapter. The resurrection of the Lord is an earnest of the fact that because He lives so shall we, not only in resurrection life beyond the grave, but in resurrection life here and now. That life which had been sown in the grave is seen arising in a new and wondrous manifestation that He had truly said, "I am the Life." The death that He died He died unto sin once, but the life which He lives He lives unto God, and because He lives so do we. How do we live in Christ? In the very beginning of things (Genesis 1:29) the fruit of the ground was given unto man for his need, and in due course we have corn referred to as the main sustenance of man. Natural men could indeed live by bread alone, but as God is dealing with spiritual things under a disguise of natural ones, we must look for the spiritual counterpart, and we find it in the words of God through

Moses: "Man doth not live by bread alone, but by every thing that proceedeth out of the mouth of the LORD doth man live" (Deuteronomy 8:3).

Moses was exhorting the people in view of their life in Canaan, that land which would produce corn in abundance, that land which is the type for us of resurrection-life as we may know it here. But Moses looks back, and says firstly, "He humbled thee ... and fed thee with manna ... that He might make thee know that man doth not live by bread alone ...." The manna is thus set before us in its significance as food from God. Now in Leviticus 23. we have a reference back to this very subject of the manna, for the word for "sheaf" is the same as the word "omer" which is used in connection with the manna, and is not used much elsewhere than in Exodus 16 and Leviticus 23. Since "An omer is a tenth part of an ephah" (Exodus 16:36), the meal-offering of Leviticus 23 is thus measured in omers, and an omer is a man's eating (Exodus 16:16,18,22).

It is indeed most remarkable that the Lord Jesus should have brought these matters in close association again in His discourse in John 6. The "true bread from heaven" (verse 32) was Himself. "I am the bread of life" (verse 48). "The bread which I shall give is My flesh, for the life of the world" (verse 51, and also verse 33). What the Lord had in view was life in men, a life which could not be sustained without proper provision, and that provision was to be found in Himself. The eating of Himself as the Bread of Life is not that life might accrue, but that it might be maintained in richer fruition, expanding in the service of faith, and overflowing in life to the service of Heaven. Life eternal is to know God and His Son, even the Lord Jesus, and it is only found in abundance, with a true zest of living, as it is nourished by the Bread of Heaven. And that Bread from Heaven is also called the Life and the Word of God by which men live. But as we eat of Him we become partakers of Him, sharers in His life, and in us will be manifested those things which made His life so beautiful, for the visible life of the Lord on earth was lived before God in the same way as ours may be.

His meat was to do the will of Him that sent Him (John 4:31). The Word of God was to Him a sure resource, a shield, His meditation day and night, His daily food: "Thy words were found, and I did eat them." Hence we gather thoughts from the meal-offering which have to do with His own life, and our life as proceeding from Him.

The principal ingredient of the meal-offering is corn, and it could be offered either in the ear as firstfruits (Leviticus 2:14), or it could be offered as fine flour (verses 1 and 4). But the natural product in the sheaf or in the ear was the lowest grade of offering, and even so it could not be offered as it came from the earth; it had to be parched with fire or bruised in the fresh ear. It was to be thus prepared in greater or less degree for its service as the food of the priests, and it is thus an appealing symbol of the One who knew the bruising of His service on earth that He might be so acquainted with all our sorrows and sufferings as to be indeed fitted to nourish us in all our need.

The fine flour had to be perfectly ground, but it is no part of the offering to do the grinding, for the flour was brought already perfected into fineness. The Lord was always perfect. Nevertheless, if the grindstones or the fire have not been in evidence, there is the unalterable fact that their efforts were seen in the finished product. We may not see the processes of the perfecting of the Lord (Hebrews 5:7-9) yet we know that such things as He learned on earth are the means of blessing to us now. Three other ingredients, oil, frankincense and salt, were regarded as essential parts of the meal-offering, while in contrast to these, two materials, honey or leaven, must not be incorporated in any way. The oil could be poured on to the offering or the cakes could be anointed with it. There can be no hesitation as to the meaning of this, for the Lord Jesus was anointed with the Holy Spirit, as in Luke 3:22 and 4:1 and many other references.

The frankincense is a symbol of purity or fragrance, and the fire of the altar brings out its sweet savour. Honey and leaven are symbols of corruption; in spite of the sweetness of the honey it soon ferments and it does not stand the fire. The salt is a preservative, and is used to symbolise endurance or perpetuity because of this (see Leviticus 2:13 and Numbers 18:19). These all have such obvious relationships to the Lord Jesus that further comment Is needless. When we are the offerers, and bring to God something concerning the life of the Lord it is just as essential that our offering be with the Spirit, that it be free from the honey-sweetness and the leavening of this world, and that there is about it something of "the salt of the covenant" and the frankincense which will be a sweet savour to God. Our feeding upon the Bread from Heaven also should be conducted in the same spirit that God may also have His pleasure and memorial.

CHAPTER SEVEN: THE DUTIES OF THE OFFERER

Having considered the components of the offerings we can now turn our attention to the duties performed by the offerer himself, and we find that these are given in great detail and variety. The first duty of the offerer is clearly that of assuring himself that his offering is indeed without blemish, and that he is offering according to the ordinances; otherwise he might suffer a refusal. The law was most stringent in this respect, and we know how God, through Malachi, condemned those who dishonoured Him by offering the blind and lame or sick. No man would ever think of bringing such blemished offerings if he clearly understood the purpose of the next duty laid upon him, for in most, but not all, cases he was commanded to lay his hand upon the head of the offering.

This gesture is, of course, associated in thought with the practice of "laying on of hands" in Apostolic days. It implied identification and association, so that the offerer who laid his hand upon the head of an animal was caused to realise that this animal was being accepted for him, to make atonement for him. Only the best of the herd or the flock could be deemed worthy of being offered if there was to be assurance of acceptance, and if the need for atonement was fully understood. As offerers of the present day, our joy is this, that our Offering was indeed the best, the Flower of the race, the only unblemished One that ever lived. On Him our hand is metaphorically laid, the One who stood in our room to make atonement for us. The only exception to this rule is in connection with the turtledoves, if indeed we can regard it as an exception, seeing the birds must be carried in the hand. The same might also be said of the meal-offering.

The matter next in importance to the offerer was the death of the offering. In all cases where an animal is offered it was essential that he should at least witness its death. In the higher grades of offerings it is stated that the offerer himself must kill the animal, and in the lower grades the priest acts for the offerer. It will be helpful to note that the pronoun "he" in practically all cases refers to the offerer; the words "the priest" or "the priests" are repeated wherever required. If

Leviticus 1 be carefully read through this will be clear; for instance, "he" in verse 9 must still be the offerer as "priests," not "the priest" are referred to in verse 8.

The following summary of the law as to the death of the animal will be useful.

- The burnt-offering: (1) the bullock before the LORD (1:5) at the door of the tent of meeting; (2) the sheep or goat on the northward side of the altar before the LORD (1:11); (3) (the turtledoves, by the priest, at the altar).
- The peace-offering: all grades at the door of the tent of meeting, before the LORD (3:1-2; 7-8; 12-13).
- The sin-offering: (1) the bullock (for the priest or congregation) before the LORD at the door of the tent of meeting (4:4,15). (2) the goat (for the ruler) and the female goat or lamb (for one of the people) "in the place where they kill the burnt-offering" (4:24,29,33): that is, as (2) for the burnt-offering above.
- The guilt-offering: (1) as for the sin offering (5:6). (2) (turtle-doves, by the priest).

We note at once that the animals for the higher grades of the burnt-offering and sin-offering were killed "before the LORD" and "at the door of the tent of meeting," while the animals for the lower grades were to be killed "on the northward side of the altar" though also "before the LORD." In both cases the emphasis is on the phrase "before the LORD." It must indeed have been most solemnising to know that He was indeed watchful of all that was done. There is increased emphasis laid upon this in connection with the higher grades. While all the offerings were slain "at the altar" or "in the place where they kill the burnt-offering," we must give weight to the choice of words in connection with the higher grades—they were killed "at the door of the tent of meeting." Extra emphasis is thus laid upon the solemnity of the place.

We must also note that it is the sin-offerings for the priest and for the whole congregation which receive this preferential treatment. There is something peculiarly solemn about the sin of a priest or the sin of the whole of God's saved people, and it was needful that there should be a corresponding appreciation of the intense interest of God in the atoning sacrifice. These matters have teaching for ourselves. Our offering is Christ, and we are called upon week by week to remember Him, to proclaim His death. We have not stood at the foot of the Cross in verity, to witness with horror the death of the Victim, to realise in His agony the dreadful fact of sin and its penalty, but in faith we can take our stand there, and we can clasp our hands in horror and shed tears of sorrow as we gaze upon Him. If such were our reactions to the remembrance we should know the true solemnity of our being gathered together.

The whole assembly needs to appreciate in the presence of God the fact that Christ has died. Whether we are concerned at the moment with Him as sin-offering or as burnt-offering is immaterial to this consideration, but this we know, that as God has looked with a searching eye on the agonies of the Sin-bearer, so also He looks upon that which we present. We can take our gaze, as it were, from the door of the tent of meeting and be taken up with the northward side of the altar, but we shall lose by it. There are two definite aspects, therefore, of the remembrance which seem to be linked together in this way, to be placed, so to speak, on equal footing, in the similarities between the procedure for the burnt-offering and the sin-offering.

Whether we are taken up with the sin-offering aspect or the burnt-offering aspect, it is most desirable that our hearts should be touched with the fact and the manner of the death of our Lord Jesus Christ. It is as essential to the one as to the other, and it is thus erroneous to consider the remembrance of the death as pertaining only to the offering for sin. The next duty of the offerer is to discriminate between the parts of the offering, as follows:

- The burnt-offering: (1) the bullock, sheep, or goat, had to be flayed and cut into pieces, and the inwards or legs had to be washed with water. (2) the turtle-doves had to be rended by the wings, but not divided asunder, and the crop and filth had to be taken away.
- The peace-offering: the offerer removes the fat, which is God's portion.
- The sin-offering: as in the peace-offering.
- The burnt-offering, in its higher grades, required the offerer to inspect

each part of the offering. Not one single thing that could be counted as defiling could be allowed to go with the rest on the altar.

As we contemplate Him who was the true Burnt-offering we shall look in vain for anything of defilement. We can consider the head, the eyes, the inwards, and we find His thoughts, His walk, His affections spotless indeed, for they were continually kept by Him unspotted from the world. Every type of Him, whether it be Aaron or the burnt-offering, needed to be washed to correspond with Him in His purity, and all that He Himself offers up as a sweet savour to God is washed by the word of God, as it is written of the Church (Ephesians 5. 26), "that He might sanctify it, having cleansed it by the washing of water with the word."

As we speak with God of Him who gave Himself, it is given unto us to survey every detail of the offering, and return God's word to Himself as to this perfect Man that He is truly "very good." Very little of this is seen by some who only consider the Lord Jesus as the innocent man slain on Calvary. His excellencies are unknown or undiscriminated by them, corresponding to the offering of turtle-doves, and the meagreness of that done concerning them.

It is interesting to see that in the case of the peace-offering only the fat is removed. This is God's portion, of which we shall have to say more in a later chapter. The sin-offering is on the same footing as the peace-offering in this respect. The fat, of course, speaks of the inward excellency of the offering. Turning now to the meal-offering, the offerer has principally to pour the oil on the offering and add the frankincense. This duty could not be delegated to the priest. So far as we are concerned this is an important duty as we remember before God the Lord Jesus as the Bread of Life. It is given unto us so to act by the Spirit that by His unction our remembrance of Christ ascends as a sweet savour offering. Thus we see that many of the lessons we learn from the duties of the offerer are intimately associated, if we are wise enough to see it thus, with the weekly remembrance of the Lord Jesus.

It is true that the death that He died, He died unto sin once, but week by week it is given to us to remember His death and to declare His excellency as we may see Him in His work as sin-offering, peace-offering, meal-offering, or burnt-offering. Our discriminatory powers are most exercised in the last, the highest form of offering, and happy and blessed are we, and sweet our gathering before God, when we can rise to the expression of the excellencies of Christ.

CHAPTER EIGHT: THE DUTIES OF THE PRIESTS

The nature of the priest's office was such that he was called upon to handle holy things, and to appreciate, to a degree much greater than that experienced by the offerer, the character of the offering and the character of Him to whom it was offered. The priest, as a successor to Aaron, was in his office a type of Christ so that we shall expect to find much in his duties which will cause us to appreciate the present work of the great Priest on high, while at the same time he and his fellows, in their priesthood, were a type of that priesthood in which we are found by the grace of God.

If we read carefully we shall see that in general the officiating priest is called "the priest," and that certain duties appear to have been collectively performed by "Aaron's sons, the priests." Compare, for example, Leviticus 1:5,7,8 with verse 9. Now in the book of Leviticus we have the expression "Aaron the priest" and it is desirable to ascertain, if possible, the respective parts played by Aaron and his sons. Numbers 3:3-4 refers to the sons of Aaron which were anointed, two of whom died without children, while of the remaining two we read, "Eleazar and Ithamar ministered in the priest's office in the presence of Aaron their father." It would therefore appear that while Aaron was alive his sons had in no sense an independent office and that his presence was a necessity.

Leviticus 6:20 refers to a meal offering which Aaron and his. sons had to offer in the day of his anointing, with a similar provision in verse 22 for the anointed priest that was in Aaron's stead. Now in Leviticus 9 we have this day of anointing over by 7 days, and the first duties of the priests are specified in detail. Compare verses 8 and 9, for instance, in which Aaron slew the calf and his sons presented the blood to him for his further duties. See also verses 12 and 18 which also show that Aaron's sons acted together in presenting to him the blood. In verse 20 they put the fat upon the breasts, but Aaron burnt it. We must therefore conclude that in the details of the general offerings it is well to note the references to the priests in their collective capacity, and to note also that "the priest" speaks of Aaron.

We can summarise the work of the priests as follows:

- The burnt-offering: (a) they present the blood of the bullock and sprinkle the blood round about the altar (1:5), put fire and wood on the altar (1:7), and lay the pieces in order upon it (1:8); (b) in connection with the offering from the flock, they sprinkle the blood; (c) in connection with the fowls, they do nothing.
- The peace-offering: (a) for an offering from the herd, they sprinkle the blood and they burn the fat of the offering; (b) for an offering from the flock, they sprinkle the blood.

It should be noted that the priests are not mentioned at all in connection with the sin and trespass offerings, and they have no duties in connection with the meal-offering except to receive it (2:2), (and of course afterwards to partake of it, which is not part of our present consideration). We also note that some of the duties done by the priests collectively in the higher grades of the burnt-offering and peace-offering are not performed by them in the cases of the lower grades, but in these instances the work is done only by "the priest," and in the lowest grade of the burnt-offering they do nothing. There must be some teaching in this for the priesthood of this day. It would seem quite right and proper that in connection with sin and trespass the offerer deals only with "the priest," who makes atonement for him. In this matter no priesthood can meddle.

The work of the priesthood is thus found entirely in connection with the sweet savour offerings. It was the privilege of the priests to stand with Aaron round the altar and share in the joy of the ascending offering, but whether they shared in the work of burning or not, one duty was laid upon them—they had to present the blood and to sprinkle it upon the altar that was at the door of the tent of meeting. In the great sacrifice of Christ of which all these offerings speak, there was, of course, no priesthood. That which was done was done by Him alone, and in His own person He performed all the functions of offering, offerer, priesthood and priest. If the priesthood is to be interpreted for us it must be in association with the remembrance of these things. Just as God took pleasure, to some extent at least (and not forgetting such Scriptures as Hebrews 10:6), in the sacrifices of old, because they were anticipative of the pleasure He would find in the offering up of Christ, so also He takes pleasure in that which can now be offered in the remembrance of that which has taken place.

The Levitical teaching as to the duties of the priesthood, however, shows that the true function of a holy priesthood is found in the rendering of a sweet savour offering unto God. They are seen associated with the High Priest in connection with the burnt-offering and not with a sin-offering. While we must, of necessity, remember the blood which cleansed us from our sins, so that the remembrance of the blood of Christ is precious both to God and to us in whatever aspect Christ may be considered, we must realise and remember that this is ever a preliminary to the high and holy privilege of rendering sweet savour offerings. Further, the cup of remembrance is called by the Lord the cup which is a new covenant in His blood. The first covenant (Hebrews 9:18) was associated with the sprinkling of the blood of sweet savour offerings (Exodus 24:5-8).

Note very carefully that this sprinkling was not done with the blood of sin-offerings. That covenant was a covenant of service, and the true service of the sanctuary was seen in the ascending offerings. The last covenant, in the blood of Christ, is equally a covenant of service, and this is what the Lord intended us to realise." All that the LORD hath spoken will we do" was the cry of the people of Israel, and on that basis, additional to the fact of their being redeemed, they were sprinkled with the blood. If, therefore, the blood of the sin-offering needed to be offered and accepted for the forgiveness of sin, the blood of the burnt-offering and of the peace-offering was needed for service. If a holy priesthood forgets that its principal function is to keep before God the memorial of the sacrifice which ascended to God as a sweet savour, it will enter upon a very barren state of service.

If that holy priesthood is more taken up with the remembrance of the blood that was shed at the doors of the houses in Egypt than with the remembrance of the blood of Him that gave Himself without spot or blemish as a sweet savour to God, then that priesthood will have decried its privileges and debased its office. Alas, many believers are in heart hardly over the thresholds of the doors of Egypt, and in consequence the service of God which should ascend as a sweet memorial of Christ is but an egotistical remembrance of the blessings accrued to them from the death of the lamb of the LORD's passover. To remember Him who freely offered up Himself, we must in measure be prepared to forget ourselves.

One other important duty fell to the sons of Aaron. As we scan the above list of duties we see that only in two cases do they have any part in connection with the burning. In the case of the highest grade of heart-offering they lay the pieces in order on the wood and fire and "the priest" actually burns the whole offering (1:9). But in the highest grade of peace-offering (3:1-5) there is no mention whatever of "the priest" and Aaron's sons burn the offering (verse 5). This is unique and commands our attention. In the lower grades of peace-offerings the priest takes a part. Now we have repeatedly stated that the higher grades of offerers are associated with the higher appreciation of the purpose of the offering, and here we see the priesthood exercising itself in duties that normally belong to the priest. Why should this be so in this case? The answer is that the peace-offering is peculiarly a communion offering, and more parties are concerned in it than in any other offering, for God, the priest, the priests, the offerer, his family, his friends, all can have a portion in this.

What a delight it must be to the Lord to stand aside, so to speak, and see an instructed priesthood being exercised to the utmost in priestly work in connection with that communion for which He suffered and died! Rest and peace we share with God, and. as we understand the value of it in our own souls we are a blessing to ourselves, to our family, and to our friends. The peace of God passes all understanding, and it is given to a holy priesthood to cause the expression of it to go up as a sweet savour to God, for Glory to God in the highest is associated with, and on earth peace among men in whom He is well pleased.

CHAPTER NINE: THE WORK OF THE PRIEST

The functions of the priest were of the greatest importance in connection with the people of Israel, not only in connection with the sacrifices and offerings, and the things of the Sanctuary, but also in connection with the morals and health of the people. With this wide range of activity we cannot deal, and this chapter must be limited to the work of the priest in connection with the burning of the offerings. His duties relative to the blood will be discussed in a later chapter. The priest, as we showed in the previous chapter, is the High Priest, Aaron and his successors, and therefore is a type of the Lord, so that an understanding of the priest's duties should help us to a fuller appreciation of the work of the great Anti-type. For He is a Priest on behalf of His people, and His priestly work began after His death on the Cross: "Having been made perfect ... named of God a High Priest" (Hebrews 5:10). His work is "within the veil, whither as a forerunner Jesus entered for us, having become a High Priest forever ..." (Hebrews 6:19-20).

This High Priest, like all the earthly priests, must have "somewhat to offer" (Hebrews 8:3), and that which He has offered has been the testimony of the sacrifice of Himself (Hebrews 9:14,26), the testimony of His blood (Hebrews 9:12), but that which He now offers includes our sacrifice of praise, through Him, the fruit of lips making confession to His name (Hebrews 13:15). Unless, therefore, there is a response on our part we are falling short of our privileges. One of the principal duties of the priest, in connection with the sweet savour offerings, was to perform the actual burning, whether it be of the whole as for the burnt-offering, or the handful for the meal-offering, or the fat as in the peace-offering. The word "burn," used in connection with the sweet-savour offerings, is different from that used in connection with the sin-offerings. In the latter case it is the word for burning in the ordinary sense, but in the former case it is a word used in association with incense.

The priest has in mind, not the burning up as destruction, but the burning which is regarded as a means to produce a sweet smell. Whether the appreciation of the offerer was made known in the highest grade or the lowest grade of offering, it is the priest who burnt the offering, and the worth of the sacrifices of praise which we render, the value of the appreciation of the great offering which was Christ, the discernment of His excellencies, the testimony of His blood, all reach unto God through Him and it is He who gives value to them and causes them to ascend as a sweet savour. It has been reiterated that in the lowest grades of offerings the offerer does very little indeed, and the priest does more. The priest, therefore, makes up for the deficiency of the offerer. The offering itself is perfect, and the sweet savour has no degrees of sweetness—all is sweet to God who receives it. But in the higher grades of offerings the priest does less and the offerer is thus accorded the privilege of doing more, to his own spiritual welfare.

The One who can take the unuttered groanings of His saints or can translate them into fervent supplications on their behalf before the face of His Father can, and does, take the meagre offerings and adds His own sweetness to them. But it is ever His desire to set with joy before God the richness of our utterings, the testimony of spiritual life in us. An analogy may help: the ungrammatical writings of a contributor may be polished by an editor, but it is a pleasure when the contributions are so well expressed that they can be passed into print untouched. So, I take it, the Lord has delight when we do more in our spiritual enlightenment and He is called upon to do less. As we pointed out in the last chapter, this finds its highest expression, so far as we are concerned, in the burning of the highest grade of the peace-offering, when the priest in one sense is not seen to act, though, be it noted, all is done in his presence, as we saw in connection with the priestly work of the sons of Aaron.

Reverting to the matter of burning, we must take care to distinguish between two separate acts of burning required for the offerings for sin. Part of the sin offering, namely, the fat, had to be burned on the altar of burnt offering, exactly as in the case of the peace-offering. Here the word used is 'qatar' as is used in connection with the sweet-savour offerings (Leviticus 4:10, 19,26,31,35; also in 5:12, for the handful of meal), so that these portions are burned as having fragrance, but the words "for a sweet savour of rest" are not added. Just as the sin-offering needed to be perfect, so also the fat, the emblem of inward health, had to be perfect, and God appreciated the perfection as a fragrance.

The perfection of Christ as an offering for sin was gratifying indeed to God. But the animal itself had to be burned (saraph) elsewhere, outside the camp (e.g. 4:12), because it was offered for sin, and had to suffer the emblem of divine wrath. Yet even so, any place without the camp would not do, and this brings us to another part of the work of the priest. It was part of the priest's duties to care for the ashes of the sweet savour offerings (6:10-11), which had to be placed first of all beside the altar, where also, "beside the altar, on the east part, in the place of the ashes" (1:16) were placed the crop and filth of the fowls used for burnt-offerings. The priest had thereafter to carry the ashes to a clean place outside the camp and it was to this place that he had to carry the sin-offerings.

One would have thought that someone other than the high priest would have done this laborious and even menial work, but it was only the anointed priest who could so act. How solemnising is the thought that sin should cause one so high to stoop so low! How perfect the picture of One who was prepared for the lowest stoop in order to cope with the consequences of sin! Here, in this clean place, the sin-offering was burned, and the ashes mingled with the ashes of the burnt-offering. The great care shewn in connection with these ashes must have some significance for us, and the mingling of the ashes was apparently deliberate. The whole pile, perhaps, would speak of the completion of the great work of Christ, as sin-offering, but also as burnt-offering, which brought forth the words, "It is finished."

It was one offering, one sacrifice, which we have viewed in different aspects, and when all was over that perfect body was reverently laid in a clean place, and guarded by the angels of God. The fire of divine wrath was over as well as the ascending offering, and God cared for that which was left. Only the higher grades of sin offering, those for the priest and for the congregation, were burnt outside the camp. The other sin offerings were not burnt, apart from the fat, and they were used (as we shall see in a later chapter) for the food of the priests. Hebrews 13 deals with this point, that only those beasts whose blood was brought into the holy place by the high priest, as an offering for sin, were burned without the camp (verse 11). These two classes or grades of offerings are obviously associated with service and communion, and Hebrews 13:10 makes it very clear that there is no thought of personal sustenance involved in this aspect of the work on the Cross—the death of the Lord is viewed as for sanctification, as fitting for the service of the house of God (see verses 12 and 15).

So perfect is the type that we have even the suffering without the gate (verse 12) portrayed in the burning without the camp. We shall miss a great deal if this aspect of the death of the Lord is not clearly grasped, that His suffering was with a view to communion and praise. David appears to have had the same subject in mind in Psalm 36:8 and Psalm 63:4-5, for the word therein translated fatness is the same word as is used for the ashes of the altar. In the latter Psalm he refers to "fat" and "fatness" (ashes) as though considering the offering up of the fat and the completion of the sacrifices. "They shall be abundantly satisfied with the fatness of Thy House. My soul shall be satisfied as with fat [RV margin] and fatness. And my mouth shall praise Thee with joyful lips." As we contemplate the same scene, the mute witness of the great sacrifice, there should also well up in our hearts the abundance of satisfaction which results in a praising people.

CHAPTER TEN: THE SPRINKLING, POURING, AND SCATTERING OF THE BLOOD

The teaching concerning the blood of the offerings is vital to our understanding of the work of Christ, and it is with reverence that we approach a subject on which we ourselves would long for deeper knowledge. We shall firstly seek to point out some essential differences in the meanings of the words used in referring to the blood. It is to be regretted that the translators have used one English word to express two different Hebrew words, for the blood of the burnt-offering and the blood of the sin-offering, for example, are each said to be "sprinkled" though the ideas conveyed are not the same.

The word 'zaraq' is used when all the blood is to be sprinkled, and for convenience we shall express this operation by the word "scatter." The word 'nazah', which means to spirt, in small drops as with the finger, is best expressed by the word "sprinkle." In general, these two words are used with very great precision, but there is an apparently exceptional case which is helpful. In Numbers 19. the water of separation (the water added to the ashes of the red heifer) was sprinkled upon those who needed to be cleansed, and normally this word is used when the sinner was cleansed, but in verses 13 and 20 we have brought before us the cases of those who refuse to be purified, and it is then said that they were condemned because the water of separation had not been scattered upon them, as though they had refused the cleansing power of the whole of that water.

The blood of the burnt-offerings and peace-offerings was scattered by the priests, the sons of Aaron, and when Moses took the book and made a covenant with the people (Exodus 24:6,8) he scattered the blood of sweet savour offerings upon the altar, the people and the book. It is the general rule for the blood of sweet savour offerings to be scattered, the whole of it being so used, but when we have sin-offerings brought before us, a portion of the blood only is sprinkled. The instructions concerning the blood of the sin-offering are of very great interest and importance, and we shall proceed to consider these in detail. We shall deal firstly with the procedure in the cases of the sin-offerings for the sins of individuals, from a ruler downwards, and we find that in all these cases there were two distinct operations, both taking place at the altar of burnt-offering (Leviticus 4:25,30,34, and 5:9): (1) putting the blood on the horns of the altar; (2) pouring the blood at the base of the altar.

To understand the meaning of these operations we must refer to the institution of the rites of the offerings, as set forth in Leviticus 8. Thus verse 15 makes it clear that these operations have different purposes, the first being that the altar might be "purified" and the second being that it might be "sanctified," the last having in view atonement for the altar. These two ideas are at first sight so similar that we might well wonder wherein lay the difference. The thought of atonement for the altar, particularly after the anointing referred to in earlier verses, seems somewhat strange, and it is not until we investigate the word 'chata', which has been translated "purified," that we realise how much has been lost in the translation. This word means "to miss (the mark)" and from it comes the word for "trespass." Hence the thoughts associated with the putting of blood on the horns of the altar are really concerned with a trespass against the altar, whereby it becomes defiled.

In all these cases of individual sin the offerer was caused to understand that when the blood was put upon the horns of the altar it showed that there had been a missing of the mark. His sin was an offence against the altar of burnt-offering and without that altar being sanctified, and without atonement for it being made, it was unable to fulfil its primary purpose in connection with sweet savour offerings. He was caused to realise that his sin affected the altar, that while it remained unforgiven there was an effect upon the reception by God of that which was His due. The sinner may never have realised this, but when the blood was put on the horns of the altar he realised that it was unclean until it was sanctified by the pouring out of the blood of the sin-offering at the base of the altar. Then atonement was made. It is outside our present purpose to discuss the special case of the red heifer of Numbers 19., but there the consequences of uncleanness are very solemnly set forth, for even the priest who was himself "clean," and all those who were "clean," and had a share in the rites, became unclean and temporarily unfitted for service because of their services for the sins of others (verses 7,8,10). This is indeed a very solemn matter, that others should be so affected by our sins. Many believers are not sufficiently concerned in their souls as to this.

When we consider the cases of the higher grades of sin-offering, when the priest or the congregation had sinned, we have these thoughts intensified, for it is now not only the altar of burnt-offering that is affected, but the service within the Sanctuary itself. The blood had to be sprinkled before the LORD seven times, before the veil (Leviticus 4:5-6, 16-17), and then the priest had to put some of the blood upon the horns of the altar of sweet incense, that precious golden altar from which ascended to God the sweetness and preciousness of the perfume. This sprinkling of blood teaches us that the sanctuary itself had become regarded as unclean, that the altar of sweet incense had been rendered unfitted for service, because of the sin of the priest or of the congregation. The sprinkling was an acknowledgment of this solemn fact by the priest, as well as a token to God of the sacrifice that had been made and of the blood to be poured out.

If the sprinkling had been sufficient for cleansing, then the pouring out of the rest of the blood at the base of the brazen altar would have been redundant. When the blood was sprinkled it had in view that full atonement shortly to be effected, the pouring out of precious blood in expiation, the cleansing of the altar of burnt-offering thereby effected, and consequently the renewed freedom of the priest to officiate in the service of the LORD. There is far too little exercise among believers as to the effects of sin in hindering service Godward. Trespasses and sins should be dealt with by the individual without loss of time, lest his faults mar the service of a serving and worshipping people. If there was more self-examination prior to the Remembrance there would be a fuller and freer exercise before God. Alas, too many fail to realise that the dead fly in the ointment may cause the whole to send forth a stinking savour.

In our remarks on the work of the priests we made it clear that their work was principally associated with the blood of the sweet savour offerings. Their duty was not merely to sprinkle a small portion, but the whole was scattered. It would seem as though there could not be by a holy priesthood too great an apprehension of the blood of the Divine sweet-savour offering. But we often feel, as we ourselves act on Lord's Day morning in giving thanks in association with the cup, that the profoundness of the theme transcends one's powers of understanding and expression. As we listen to others, we often feel that there is a poverty of expression regarding that of which the cup speaks. Too often, what is then offered up in thanksgiving is but a second edition of that which was said earlier in association with the loaf, or else it would appear as though what had been left unsaid on the first occasion is said on the second. It is also sometimes the case that what was said concerning the cup might equally have been said concerning the loaf, and vice-versa.

To our mind, this is wrong. The message of the loaf is not the message of the cup, and if the peculiar teaching and significance of the cup is not appreciated and expressed then the services unto God will be on a low plane. The cup which reminds us of the new covenant in the blood of Christ should cause us to realise the tremendous value of that blood whereby we, even we, are enabled to draw near and speak unto God in full communion. The fact that we, in view of what we once were, are enabled to come with boldness into the very presence of God is of tremendous and fascinating importance. The privileges which we have should stagger us. We know that we are clean, but we cannot fathom the deep mystery of the means whereby we are clean. No wonder the poet could sing, "And can it be, that I should gain, An interest in the Saviour's blood?", nor that he should exclaim, "'Tis mystery all; the Immortal dies!" With great diffidence have we sought to pen these few thoughts on this great subject, but it is our hope that there may be an exercise among brethren as to the importance of that which is brought before us in the cup.

CHAPTER ELEVEN: THE FOOD OF THE PRIESTS

Just as the Book of Deuteronomy, in its second statement of the Law of God, gives us oft-times a fresh view of Divine principles, so also in the Book of Leviticus do we find a second summary of the ordinances relating to the offerings, and each part of this section, from Leviticus 6:8 to 7:38, opens with similar words, as "This is the law of the burnt-offering," etc. One would have thought that the earlier chapters would have given the law as to these matters. But now the whole subject is being reviewed from an entirely fresh angle; whereas chapters 1 to 6:7 are to the people of Israel (see 1:2), the second section is to Aaron and his sons (6:9). Many of the details of the instructions are extremely interesting, but we shall have to pass over them, and discuss the most important matter here touched on.

It becomes increasingly clear as we read the section that it is principally taken up with the subject of the food of the priests. Another matter which immediately engages our attention is that the peace-offering is relegated to the end, and is referred to in greater detail than any other offering. Further, the emphasis is laid on the holy character of the sin-offering. In fact, as we see from 6:25, 7:7, and also 6:17, the sin-offering is said to be "most holy" and even the meal offering is to be regarded as "most holy" in the same sense as the sin-offering. This is a complete reversal of emphasis from what we get in the first five chapters. There the burnt-offering is supreme and the sin-offering is said to be dealt with "in the place where they kill the burnt-offering." In those early chapters it is the thought of the sweet savour which is the basis of grouping, but in this later section it is the thought of the provision for the priests which determines the order of treatment; thus we get:

> (1) The burnt-offering treated first, which provides food neither for the priests nor for the offerer;

> (2) then the meal offering, sin-offering, and guilt-offering, which provide food only for the males of the sons of Aaron (6:18, 6:29, 7:6, 7:10);

(3) lastly, the peace-offering, which provides food, not only for the offerer, and the males of the Aaronites, but also for the females.

If we examine some exceptions to the general rules of the offerings grouped under (2) above, we get a little more insight into the principles of interpretation. It appears from Leviticus 6:23 and 30 that certain meal offerings and sin-offerings could not be eaten because they were to be wholly burnt, and on considering the references back to the sin-offerings we find that the exceptional cases pertain to

(a) the meal-offering for the priest himself;

(b) the sin-offering for the sin of the anointed priest;

(c) the sin-offering for the whole congregation.

If we take it that of these three the first two cannot find fulfilment in the antitype of the anointed priest (that is, in the Lord) we are led to consider the last one and we see from Hebrews 13:12, which refers to this, that because the body of the animal was burnt then the priests could not find sustenance in the offering made for the sin of the congregation. So also we must not look to the One offering made for the sin of the whole people as that which is referred to in connection with the food of the priests. We are forced, therefore, to consider that the priests found sustenance in the offerings made for the individual sins of the rulers and the people. It seems to be a very strange thing that the sin-offerings should be used for food at all, and stranger still that the bodies and the food had to be handled and eaten with the utmost reverence.

As sinbearers they were doomed to death and bore in their bodies the penalties that came from God's abhorrence of sin. But once the death had been accomplished the bodies were put under very special care. We saw something of this same principle in connection with the work of the priest, how he carried out of the camp to a clean place the bodies of animals offered for certain sins, and how in that clean place the ashes of the bodies were mingled with the ashes of the burnt-offerings. Here, in the case of other sin-offerings, whosoever touched the bodies must be holy (see 6:25-30), any garment affected by such bodies must be washed in a holy place, the earthen vessel used to cook the flesh could not be afterwards used and must be broken, and any brazen vessel must be thoroughly cleansed after use. The actual eating must also be done in a holy place, the court of the tent of meeting. We might well ask the meaning of all this.

The fire of divine wrath which fell on Christ when He became the Sin-bearer lasted not a moment after His death. Thereafter His body was an object of reverence on earth, and will be so forever in heaven. The object of awe on the Cross is the theme of joy and wonder here. Another important point in connection with the eating of the sin-offering is that only the males of the house of Aaron could eat of it (6:29), whereas the peace-offering could be eaten by males and females (7:32 and 10:14). We are caused to realise that this distinction is of very great importance. The sacrifices of peace-offerings are not said to be "most holy" as are the others just referred to, and they need not be eaten in a holy place. We must conclude that the eating of the "most holy" sacrifices had something to do with ceremonial satisfaction, if we may so put it.

The males, as active members, are seen eating together in a holy place of the "most holy" sacrifices. There is a measure of solemnity about it. We would judge that much the same sort of satisfaction is associated with those occasions when the sins of an individual are confessed and the Assembly shares in the joy of knowing that the sin has been confessed, and the reproach against the Testimony is removed. When the individual's sin was regarded as a trespass against the altar, it must have been a source of joy to the priesthood to know that the matter was rectified, and there was a collective sharing in the satisfaction of atonement.

A very interesting and important revelation is made in Leviticus 10:17 as to the meaning of these ordinances concerning the food of the priests. On the day of consecration of Aaron and his sons a goat had been offered up for the people as a sin-offering. It was not offered for an offering for collective sin, for in that case a bullock (4:13) would have had to be offered, and the blood of the bullock would have had to be presented in the sanctuary, while the body would not have been used for food at all. But a goat was offered for the people, and as Moses points out to Aaron (10:18), because the blood was not brought into the sanctuary then the body should have been eaten by the priests. Moses further reveals (10:17) that it was given to the priests for food that it might bear (or take away) the iniquity of the congregation, to make atonement for them.

This is something new and profound. We can only conclude that the priests thus had a solemn responsibility laid upon them. As we have said previously, the priests had no share in the ordinances relating to the sacrifice of the offering, they neither touched it nor sprinkled the blood. Only the priest could act to forgive sin, but the priests in eating the sacrifice found satisfaction in the accomplished work. It is well-pleasing indeed to God when the priesthood thus finds satisfaction. The reason why Aaron and his sons could not eat the sin-offering on the occasion referred to was that in the interval between the atonement made by the sin-offering and the eating of the body further grievous sin had resulted, so that there could not have been any satisfaction in completing a rite which had ceased to have reality. There could have been no joy over a sin atoned for when the cloud of a more grievous sin had overshadowed the priesthood.

In the interpretation for the priesthood of this day we must conclude that we are to find holy and collective satisfaction in Christ as the Offering made for individual sin. The consideration of this should indeed be a continual source of satisfaction, and ought to tend, as the contemplation of Christ ever should (see Ephesians 4:12-13) toward the upbuilding of "the body." It should be an act of satisfaction to the collective people of God when the sins of believers are confessed and forgiven before God, so that the interpretation for us today of the eating of the sin-offering is that the provision for sin made by God in the Person of His Son should cause us to be filled and strengthened in the collective sense.

As regards the meal-offering, we have already commented so we shall not enter into details. But it may be noted that, as in the case of the sin-offering, it was "most holy" and that only the males of the house of Aaron could eat of it (6:18). We pointed out in connection with the meal offering that in the Festivals of Jehovah the peace-offering comes last, the same order precisely as that which we have in this portion of Leviticus. Communion could only commence in its fullness after the cross-work was over, and this can be either a collective matter, in the solemnity of the priestly work of the Assembly, or a family matter as those in the family of God. Hence the daughters of Aaron and his sons are seen to share in the peace-offerings. What they ate was a due for ever to the Aaronic priests from the children of Israel.

There is undoubtedly much joy and gladness and upbuilding power in the blessing to the individual saint in his communion with God in connection with the great Peace-offering, but there is a sense in which the whole assembly gets its portion from this also, just as the priests and their families shared with the offerer and with God in the sacrifices of peace-offerings.

The Food of the Offerer

In association with the preceding subject, we should also consider the food of the offerer. It is only in the peace-offering that the offerer finds a portion, and it is only as we contemplate the peace which we have in Christ that as individuals we can know the true peace of God which passes all understanding. Such a state of mind calls for thanksgiving, and the spirit that is enjoined to the offerer is that in which the full savour of this thanksgiving is enjoyed without stint. So we read that none of it shall be left until the morning (7:15). With it was to be offered a meal-offering, and our minds go back to the ordinance concerning the manna—none of it could be left until the morning. The thankful heart should not consider it necessary to save some of his elation until the morrow. Some of us are perhaps, too much of this stingy spirit, so that we fail to enter into the full joy of thanksgiving for the peace we have in Christ.

With regard to the peace-offering for a vow the ordinances are different and solemn. Whereas thanksgiving should well up in our hearts day by day, a vow (or freewill offering) is a rare occurrence. What solemn moments have been spent before God in the deep satisfaction of peace with Him! What dedication has been made! It is permissible to continue to feed on that experience and on Him for whose sake it was given. But, alas, how many have delighted only in the dedication, the promising to oneself and to God of a life devoted to service, and yet have never achieved what they set out to do. He who vowed could feed for a "second day," but what remained over on "the third day" was to be burnt. We know that "the third day" speaks of resurrection. It will not be sufficient in that day to seek satisfaction in the great resolves of heart that once were made.

"I have found no works of thine fulfilled before my God" was the word to the saints in Sardis (Revelation 3:2), who had a name that they lived, and yet were dead. The knowledge of the peace in Christ our Lord should stimulate us to vow in our hearts to serve Him, but "when thou vowest a vow unto God, defer not to pay it ..." (Ecclesiastes 5:1-7).

CHAPTER TWELVE: THE TITHE AND THE FREE-WILL OFFERINGS

It is fitting that in closing this book we should give a little attention to the class of offerings which depended upon the blessing received from God. The offerings for sin and trespass depended upon a knowledge of the frailty and sinfulness of men, and the sweet savour offerings depended upon an appreciation of God's due from men, but the tithe was a compulsory offering demanded of men who inhabited the land by the favour of the LORD, who received blessings from Heaven above and earth beneath because of the munificence of the Creator.

"The world is Mine, and the fulness thereof" was the word of the LORD through Asaph in Psalm 50. His are all the cattle on a thousand hills, and the wild beasts also are His. When He uttered those words, God had shined forth out of Zion (verse 2), and desired His saints to be gathered together, those that had made a covenant with Him by sacrifice (verse 5). That which they had offered had come from Him in the first place, but He yearned for a spirit of thankfulness in their hearts, so that they might offer unto Him the sacrifice of thanksgiving (verses 14 and 23). Again in Psalm 24. we read, "The earth is the LORD's, and the fulness thereof" and David immediately links with this the questions, "Who shall ascend unto the hill of the LORD? And who shall stand in His holy place?" The things of earth are always related to the things of heaven, and the generation of them that seek after God, that seek the face of the God of Jacob (verse 6) is the same in heart as that of the man who stood in the loneliness of the desert place, in that fearful place where he had discerned God's House, who set up the pillar before God, and who discerned also that three things needed to be connected in his own mind:

(1) the God who gave him bread to eat and raiment to put on,

(2) the House of God, the place where respect could be paid to God, and

(3) the response of a thankful heart as shown in the vow to give a tenth unto God of all that God gave him (Genesis 28:20-22).

So in Psalm 24, the clean hands and a pure heart, a soul which has not been lifted up unto vanity and has not sworn deceitfully, are proper to the one who connects the fulness of the earth and the place of the Name.

The tithe is first mentioned in connection with Abraham and Melchizedek, priest of God Most High (Genesis 14:20 and Hebrews 7:4), King of Righteousness and King of Peace, for Abraham had been richly blessed and it was the duty of Melchizedek to indicate the source of that blessing: "Blessed be Abram of God Most High, possessor of heaven and earth." "The earth is the LORD's and the fulness thereof." We live in a day when the blessings of heaven are not seen at first-hand — for most of us are not anxiously waiting for the rain from heaven to water the land; the parched ground and the fear of famine are not seen as the withholding of God's favour. Nevertheless, when all is traced back to the Source from which it comes it is the same Hand that provides for our needs.

The Israelites were nearer to God in this—the Land was the LORD's (Leviticus 25:23). Their portion was to enjoy it, to till it, to inherit it. but it was the LORD's, and in the Law of God there is a beautiful mingling of the words, "It is thine" and "It is Mine." This acknowledgment of the claims of God upon the land and its produce was met by the tithe (Leviticus 27:30-33). This was the end of "the commandments which the LORD commanded Moses for the children of Israel in Mount Sinai" (Leviticus 27:34). The Book of Leviticus opens with the Law of the Burnt Offering and closes with the Tithe. The blessing of God was very patent; the flocks and herds, the fruits of the ground—all depended upon Him. It was a privilege and a duty to return a portion unto God. But in our day also, if we are spiritually alive it should also be evident that as we are blessed of God so also we have a duty to God. Shall I give a tithe in this day of grace and not of the Law? Why not?

We can have little sympathy with those who will argue as to the portion that is the Lord's, for the faithful Israelite was in no way limited to the tithe; he could bring his free-will offerings and set them before God. Not all burnt-offerings and sacrifices were free-will offerings, for some were compulsory. The burnt-offering was demanded by the ordinance of God from Israel unitedly, as in the daily burnt-offering and in the annual ceremonies of the Day of Atonement, and also of individuals who were unclean. The burnt-offering that was associated with the guilt-offering (Leviticus 5:9-10) was as necessary for forgiveness as the guilt-offering itself. An Israelite who walked in the fear of God would feel under perpetual obligation to bring a burnt-offering that he might fulfil the Law of God, for the same Law which said "Thou shalt not covet" and demanded a trespass-offering if the law was broken, also said, "Thou shalt love the LORD thy God," and the burnt-offering might be regarded as necessary to the demonstration of this.

Nevertheless, a sweet-savour offering was the finest possible expression of such devotion to God that led the offerer to give a free-will offering. Thus we see that we must distinguish between the necessities of our spiritual life and the privileges. "God loveth a cheerful giver," and it is as true today as ever it was that if the believer is exercised unto thankfulness, and pours out before God the expression of his appreciation of God's truthfulness and grace, then such will ascend unto God as a sacrifice of a sweet smell, an odour acceptable unto God. "Whoso offereth the sacrifice of thanksgiving glorifieth Me" (Psalm 50:23).

In bringing this book to a close we must again express our earnest hope that the results of our studies may have widened the interest of readers in the Scriptures, and that they may have found indeed that the ordinances of the law provide a rich treasury for the student. As we have dwelt on one portion after another we have felt that avenues of truth have opened up before us which would call for exploration, and new thoughts have caused us to desire opportunity to modify old ones here and there, but it is as we are conscious of the many imperfections of our own words that we become more than ever convinced of the rich perfection of the Word of God.

BOOK TWO - THE FESTIVALS OF JEHOVAH UNDER THE OLD COVENANT

CHAPTER ONE: FESTIVALS

The "Festivals of Jehovah" that we are to consider are those defined in Leviticus 23, where, as we shall see, these festivals appear to be considered in a unique way as from the standpoint of God rather than of man. They begin with the Sabbath, which festival has a weekly remembrance, whereas the remainder, seven in number, have an annual remembrance. We must distinguish between the remembrance of a thing and the thing itself. Thus the Passover was often remembered, but, as fulfilled in Christ, it only occurs once; so also Pentecost, referred to in verse 16, occurs once only in God's dealings with men, and we conclude that the things spoken of here occur once only in what we speak of as God's year. The festivals conclude with the "Festival of Tabernacles", which undoubtedly is always associated with the thought of God dwelling with His people.

These festivals have application to the Israelites in the first place, but there can be no doubt that they have application also to the redeemed in Christ. The last festival is in the seventh month, and we are told nothing as to what will follow, though we may contemplate with great profit how that God has now seated us in heavenly places in Christ Jesus, "that in the ages to come He might shew the exceeding riches of His grace in kindness toward us in Christ Jesus" (Ephesians 2:6-7). See also 1 John 3:2: "Now are we children of God, and it is not yet made manifest what we shall be." The term "festival" is rather misleading, and we shall do well to understand the meaning of the original words translated "set feasts" or "appointed seasons" in the Revised Version. Those who possess a concordance may be recommended to verify that there are two Hebrew words translated "feast" and that one of these 'chag' is derived from a word which literally means to move in a circle or to march in a sacred procession, and that wherever this word is used we have to do with the ritual enjoined upon the observers of the festival.

In Exodus 23 and 34, Numbers 28 and 29, and Deuteronomy 16, the feasts are referred to by this word chag, whereas in Leviticus 23 they are referred to by the word 'mowed', which means "an appointment" or "a fixed season." By implication the same word is used when speaking of "the tent of meeting." Hence the term "set feast" closely expresses the original word. Moreover, while we often read of "feasts" to or unto Jehovah, it is only in Leviticus 23. that the feasts are called "feasts of Jehovah" and "My set feasts." It is because of these facts that this chapter takes on a very special character. Further, notice the remarkable lists of offerings of all kinds to be offered by a sin-stained people, as given in Numbers 28 and 29, and contrast with this the fact that in the chapter before us there is only one sin-offering (verse 19) contemplated by God, and in association with that which takes place at Pentecost.

I suggest, therefore, that in Numbers the festivals are considered from the manward side and in Leviticus from the Godward side. It is worth stressing at the outset that God speaks to us in His word by omission and by reiteration. Who among us would have thought of the wonderful interpretation given as to Melchizedek, had not the Holy Spirit revealed the significance of the omission of details of his genealogy in the inspired word? So also, here, what is omitted from other accounts will give us cause for thought, and we shall be led to give due importance to such details as are given. When, in verse 2, we get "the set feasts of the LORD ... even these are My set feasts" we have reiteration which gives importance to the whole chapter. We note also that the teaching of the festivals is based on a correct interpretation of types, and we shall need to be very cautious as to this. A type helps us to understand the direct teaching of the Scriptures, and the details of the type are then sometimes of very great significance. In this chapter we shall expect every detail to be pregnant with truth, as we are under no uncertainty as to the interpretation of the type as a whole.

These appointed seasons had to be "proclaimed" to be "holy convocations." It is another profitable exercise (Acts 17:11 is commended to the diligent reader) to trace out the meanings of the words here used, and to correlate these passages with others in which the same words are used. The word used for "convocation" (miqra) is derived from qara, which is the word here translated as "proclaimed," and the phrase simply means "call out the called together." The words imply a definite calling to the people, and the manner of it is indicated in Numbers 10:2 where the same word qara is used. It is very interesting to note that one of these convocations is referred to in Nehemiah 8, and the familiar verse 8, literally translated, should read, "so that they understood the calling-together" (not "the reading"); for the word translated "reading" is the same as that translated "convocation" elsewhere.

The same word is twice used by Isaiah, and it is sad to read, "The calling of assemblies [convocations] I cannot away with ... your appointed feasts My soul hateth" (Isaiah 1:13-14); sad indeed that "My feasts" should become "your feasts" at that day and "the feasts of the Jews" at the time of our Lord on the earth (John 5:1). In contrast to this, Isaiah pictures what shall be the glory over "Mount Zion and over her assemblies [convocations]" (Isaiah 4:5). When men get taken up with the human side of a thing in which God should have His portion, it is a sad day. A festival "unto" Jehovah is what God desires, and our eyes should be on Him, whether it be in connection with the assemblies of the saints or in the study of the word of God.

CHAPTER TWO: THE SABBATH

The special importance of the Sabbath throughout the Scriptures receives peculiar emphasis in connection with the Festivals. It is by no means without significance that the Sabbath receives the first place in the Festivals of Jehovah, for "From Sabbath unto Sabbath" would fittingly describe God's year from the time of the completed creation until after all things have been made new. Let us notice that the seventh day is not called the Sabbath in verse 3, and that the seventh day is not the only day for keeping "a sabbath of solemn rest." The Festivals are usually given according to the calendar, so that they could occur on any day of the week, save the Festival of the Wave-sheaf and the Festival of the Wave-loaves (see verses 11,15,16) which are appointed to begin on the day after the Sabbath. In spite of this, the festivals of the seventh month are to be kept as "sabbaths of solemn rest"; see verses 24,32 and 39, especially noting that the Festival of Tabernacles has two such days.

We shall see later that the events commemorated in the seventh month are closely associated with the eternal rest which we shall enjoy with our Lord Jesus Christ and the Father. Moreover, please note that in all but one of the festivals (the exception being the Festival of the Wave-sheaf) it is commanded that "no servile work" or "no manner of work" be done (verses 3, 7, 8, 21, 25, 28, 30, 31, 35, 36). It is suggested, therefore, that in order to understand the Festivals of Jehovah we must enter into the meaning of the Sabbath rest. We all know that the rest of God on the seventh day of the week of creation (Genesis 2.1-3) led Him to hallow the seventh day, but it is very remarkable that the term "Sabbath" is not used until Exodus 16, though the word used for "rest" in Genesis 2 is derived from the same root as the word "sabbath."

Moreover, we do not find until then any explicit command to men to keep the seventh day as a sabbath. I do not suggest for one moment that men who walked with God prior to this did not keep the seventh day holy unto the LORD, but it is suggested that the silence of Scripture has a lesson for us to learn. The circumstances under which the seventh day is made known to us as being enjoined upon the Children of Israel are also remarkable. There had been grave murmurings, and lusting after the flesh-pots of Egypt, so that the LORD gave them the Manna. Notice that in Exodus 16:5 the people are not then told anything about the sabbath, but are simply told to gather twice the usual amount on the sixth day. After due obedience, the rulers of the congregation came and mentioned the fact to Moses. It is not until then, I say, that they were told, "Tomorrow is a solemn rest, a holy sabbath unto the LORD" (verse 23). It is characteristic of God's dealings with men that no hardship was laid upon them in the observance of the Sabbath, since He gave them food for two days, and "so the people rested" (verse 30). That which God has ever in mind, to give His elect an eternal sabbath rest, is wholly of His providing. "In the ages to come" we shall be glad to remember that all is of grace, the gift of God, not of works, that no man should glory (Ephesians 2:7-9), and this enjoyment will be precisely the same for each of us.

Wherefore the manna was given to each man the same amount (whether he gathered much or little it mattered not), an omer a head. Notice that no reason is here given to the people or to the rulers. Jehovah had commanded it to be kept unto Himself, and had given it to the people (verses 25,29). It is not until the people come to Mount Sinai, and the Law is given to them, that they are given a reason for the command to keep the Sabbath, and this reason (Exodus 20:11) is the one already known (to us): "For in six days the LORD made Heaven and Earth ... and rested the seventh day ..." It is extremely interesting to compare this account of the giving of the ten commandments with that given in Deuteronomy 5:12-15. The words of verse 15 are not given in the account in Exodus, and they constitute an additional reason for God instituting the Sabbath.

Let us clearly distinguish between these two reasons. To remember the Sabbath because the LORD enjoined it as a remembrance of His rest is a very different thing from remembering it as a memorial of the rest of the Children of God: "Thou shalt remember that thou wast a servant in the land of Egypt, and the LORD thy God brought thee out thence by a mighty hand and a stretched-out arm: therefore the LORD thy God commanded thee to keep the Sabbath." The enjoyment of peace and rest by us, as we know ourselves redeemed for ever, should give us a deeper understanding of the rest of God which He also enjoys in Christ, the rest that is a sweet foretaste of the great eternal sabbath rest. It may be here remarked, however, that the Israelites would seem to have been rather unwilling to remember the degradation associated with the land of Egypt, even though they had been so wonderfully delivered therefrom.

When the LORD had finished communing with Moses upon Mount Sinai, He gave him the two tables of stone, and the last words uttered prior to this act (Exodus 31:12-18) are about the Sabbath: "Verily ye shall keep my sabbaths: for it is a sign between Me and you throughout your generations; that ye may know that I am the LORD which sanctify you." Please note the words we have emphasized. The place here given in the Divine communications with Moses shows again the great importance that the LORD attached not only to the sabbath, but also to the remembrance of it by His People. Here we have essentially a third reason for the remembrance (the first two reasons being connected with the creation and with redemption), that week by week the people of God might be led to give practical expression to the truth of sanctification. The knowledge (or understanding) of the purposes of God associated with this sign ought indeed to have had a tremendous spiritual influence on the people, and to have led them to value this covenant (verse 16).

Yet one of the principal reasons given for the carrying away of the people of Israel into captivity was the profanation of the Sabbath. Please read, for instance, Nehemiah 13:15-22, Jeremiah 17:19-27, Ezekiel 20:13. During this time of captivity and affliction God spoke concerning the people and the land of His choice that they should be in captivity "until the land had enjoyed her sabbaths: for as long as she lay desolate she kept sabbath" (2 Chronicles 36:21; see also Leviticus 26:34-35,43). The same thought in connection with the land is brought out in the commandments concerning the Sabbatic Year (Leviticus 25:1-6), that seventh year which was to be a year of solemn rest for the people and the land (see verse 5). Again, after seven sabbaths of years (Leviticus 25:8), the fiftieth year, the Year of Jubilee, was to be kept as a sabbath (verse 11). We will discuss the Year of Jubilee in a later chapter, and perhaps we have said sufficient for the present to provoke thought concerning this very important matter.

Believers in this dispensation are not enjoined to keep the seventh day as a sabbath to Jehovah, but the day is coming when all the earth and its inhabitants shall keep holy the Sabbath. " It shall come to pass, that from ... one Sabbath to another, shall all flesh come to worship before Me, saith the LORD" (Isaiah 66:23). In a more blessed way, however, will the Sabbath be enjoyed in that which is spoken of in Colossians 2:16-17, for the Sabbath Day is but a shadow of one of the good things to come, which things we now enjoy in measure in their various aspects, but which we shall enjoy in all their fulness in eternity. "There remaineth, therefore, a sabbath rest for the people of God " (Hebrews 4: 9), and an understanding of the close reasoning of the Epistle to the Hebrews concerning rest in its various aspects is of the profoundest practical importance to all believers.

"Today, if ye shall hear His voice, harden not your hearts" (Hebrews 3:15). The rest that comes from a knowledge of redemption is a rest indeed, yet along with it men may harden their hearts, and give no heed to the voice of the living God. The wilderness with God is a far better place than Egypt with all its burden and woe, and the redemption song can be sung and resung there, but the Promised Land is better than all; yet the redeemed could not enter in because of disobedience (Hebrews 3:18). We learn that there is a rest associated with a place. As Moses said in Deuteronomy 12:9, "Ye are not as yet come to the rest and the inheritance"; here the word translated "rest" is the same as is used in Psalm 95:11 and in Psalm 132:8,14: "They should not enter into My rest" ... "Arise, O LORD, into Thy resting place; Thou, and the ark of Thy strength" ... "This [Zion] is My resting place for ever: Here will I dwell."

The place of His habitation (Psalm 132:13) is manifestly the place where He enjoyed that rest which is associated with a people in covenant relationship with Himself, and with the sacrifices with which He is well pleased. For us to enter into this is to know and to practise the truth concerning the House of God today; "Let us give diligence to enter into that rest." It is gross folly to think that it is only in millennial and eternal times that this rest can be enjoyed. If today a believer desires to please God let him ponder how far he has entered into the enjoyment of sabbath rest, not only in redemption, but also in sanctification and in service.

CHAPTER THREE: THE BEGINNING OF MONTHS

The entrance of sin into the world involved the breaking of the Sabbath rest of God, and a new beginning had to be made in bringing rest and peace, which was to be effected in Christ through His work on the Cross. It is well to be clear that the salvation of men is never to be disassociated from service to God, in the House that He has even now on earth, and in that which is to come. God's year begins with this object in view, and hence He begins with redemption in Christ, and none of the blessings of God are realised until this matter is settled, though men would begin, if they were allowed, where God leaves off.

The passover is not until the fourteenth day of the first month, and it is highly desirable in the interests of accurate thinking to be clear as to the interpretation of the first month, for some have become confused owing to their misunderstanding of the inherent differences between God's year and man's year. When the passover took place in Egypt, God said, "This month shall be unto you the beginning of months: it shall be the first month of the year to you" (Exodus 12:2). Scripture is silent as to whether the calendar formerly used by the Israelites was devised by God or man. I suggest that God did not intervene concerning the months of the year until His purposes were about to be fulfilled, just as He was silent as to the keeping of the Sabbath until at a comparatively late date in the history of the Israelites. But as He had always contemplated the Sabbath from the Creation, and as "He appointed the moon for seasons" (Psalm 104:19), so also had He contemplated redemption in Christ our Passover (Genesis 2:3 and 3:15). The word for "seasons," both here and in Genesis 1:14, is the word 'mowed' which we have already noticed as the word translated "appointed season."

When the time was ripe He issued His commands. This particular month Abib (Exodus 23:15, 34:18, etc.) was the seventh month of the year, according to the old calendar, and some have said that man's year was half over, and also that the first six months were to be blotted out, for God was making a new beginning upon a new foundation, even the Passover, and they have typically regarded these six months as the world's history from Adam to Christ. Others have interpreted the change as the cancellation of the time spent by the brick-kilns and the flesh-pots of Egypt. The latter suggestion is illogical if we consider the festivals as having to do with the whole of God's dealings with the race of Adam. Regarding the first interpretation, we must note that the beginning of God's year is not the Passover itself, but 14 "days" prior to it. We need to interpret these according to the Scriptures.

There is a certain similarity in the allocation of days in the first and seventh months. Thus each specifies the fifteenth day as the commencement of a long festival of seven or eight days. By implication, the first day of the first month has an importance corresponding to that of the first day of the seventh month, allocated to the Feast of Trumpets. In the seventh month the important Day of Atonement takes place on the tenth day, and we know that the tenth day of the first month was an important day in that the passover lamb had to be taken on that day and "kept up" until the fourteenth day (Exodus 12:3-6). This is too striking to be passed over, and I suggest that we have here something to guide us in the interpretations required.

The seventh month opens after a long interval, and God "begins" to act in a very definite and rapid manner to sum up all things, the consummation taking place when He will dwell with His people, and they shall do Him service in the place wherein is the glory of God, and the lamp thereof is the Lamb (Revelation 21:3 and 23). This is what is visualised by God from the beginning of months, and now we are able to understand what interpretation we are to put on the first day of the month, as revealed by the Scriptures in Exodus 40:2: "The LORD spake unto Moses, saying, On the first day of the first month shalt thou rear up the tabernacle of the tent of meeting." This "came to pass" (verse 17) in the second year, and we may just remark, without proof, that what takes place in the second year or month generally implies a shadow of that which takes place in God's eternal purposes. The result was that "the glory of the LORD filled the tabernacle" (verse 34).

We may now take up the point as to the rest of God at the commencement of this portion. The whole object before Jehovah is to bring about a rest associated with His resting-place. This is viewed from the commencement; the Lamb was foreknown from the foundation of the world (1 Peter 1:20); and we, who were to be blessed with every spiritual blessing, were chosen also before the foundation of the world, to the end that we should be unto the praise of His glory (Ephesians 1:3,4 and 12). Man's year is not seen by God in all this, and the history of man from Adam to Christ must rather be fitted in during the 14 days of the first month of God's year.

Now the tenth day of the month, as has been remarked, is also an important day. The number 10 is prominent in the Scriptures in connection with the testing or approving of the professed service of men, as is evident in connection with the Law, the virgins, the talents, etc. The seventh month helps us to understand the significance of the tenth day, for the Day of Atonement is a day of affliction of soul, a day of self-judging and of humbling, and a day when men on the earth will have an opportunity of revising their opinion of the man Jesus, when He comes again with power and great glory, when every eye shall see Him and men shall mourn because of Him. Again we have help from the Scriptures in the interpretation, for we read in Joshua 4:19 that the people came up out of Jordan on the tenth day of the first month, and encamped in Gilgal, and here their first act was to be circumcised. It was a day of judging and of humbling, for a covenanted people must do that which God had enjoined upon them, and no doubt the bitterness of wilderness experience was felt as they realised how far they had been out of communion with God.

The reproach of Egypt was rolled away, and they were now to enter upon that rest which they could only have in the land of Promise, a rest associated with service. Then they kept the passover. Let him that reads take heed that he understands, for Jericho was not to be attempted until they had given the proper place to the remembrance of the passover. Now the interpretation of the tenth day of the first month may be given. The Lamb of God was made manifest and men then had an opportunity of responding to the grace of God. The day of trial came and they despised the One who came to His own, and herein they judged themselves unworthy. This is the summary of the history and efforts of men, from Adam onwards, that the Lord "was in the world ... and the world knew Him not."

The Israelites, of course, knew nothing of the purposes of God as we now know them. They were content to institute a new way of reckoning the year so far as their religious ceremonies were concerned, but they never made it part of their daily lives, and to this day the Jews retain the old calendar, and their New Year is the Day of Trumpets. This is typical of men, who rarely give to the Blood of the Lamb the place it should have in their lives, as distinct from their religion. Man's year will come to a close, never to be resumed, when God begins with the events of the seventh month of His year.

We shall never be allowed to forget, when in the Glory, that the beginning of all our bliss was the death of our Lord Jesus Christ. The Israelites never knew the ways of God, but only His doings (Psalm 103:7), and even these they forgot (Psalm 78:11, 106:21). We read of the Passover being remembered for the first time in the wilderness (Numbers 9:5), then in Canaan, after which the Scriptures are silent until the days of Hezekiah (2 Chronicles 30), when his reforming zeal brought about the keeping of the passover in the second month (a matter to which I will refer to later), causing such a scene of joy as is compared to that associated with the dedication of the temple in the days of Solomon. Not again do we read of it until the time of Josiah (2 Chronicles 35 and 2 Kings 23), whose heart was tender and humble as he read the re-discovered book of the Law. What a tale of apathy and neglect is unfolded in the solemn words of 2 Chronicles 34:21 and 35:18! "Our fathers have not kept the word of the LORD, to do according to all that is written in this book ... And there was no passover like to that kept in Israel from the days of Samuel the prophet ..."

There are many precious things concerning the "keeping up" of the Lamb. This phrase is translated thus only once, from the word 'mishmereth', which is derived from a word meaning, "to hedge about, as with thorns"; that is, to guard, watch, observe, or keep, as in the expression "charge of the sanctuary," where the same word is used. It is not used, however, in the Scripture which comes to mind, "He shall give His angels charge over Thee" (Psalm 91:11), insidiously used by Satan when tempting the Lord (Luke 4:10). Note how Satan was careful to omit the words, "To keep Thee in all His ways," where the word "keep" is the primitive root (shamar) from which mishmereth is derived. This is very suggestive indeed. The Lamb of God was watched and guarded as by a hedge of thorns in all His days upon the earth and kept in all His ways. He who kept the Law in all its points observed the keeping of the passover, and some of His teaching concerning His approaching death is indicated by Him on these occasions.

There are four occasions referred to in the Gospels:

(1) Luke 2:41. "Wist ye not that I must be in My Father's House?"

(2) John 2:13-24. See also 1:29,35,43, and 2:1, and the "not many days" of 2:12, showing that the Lord commenced His public work only a few days before the passover. One might even ask, Was it on the tenth day that John said, "Behold, the Lamb of God"? Note, too, verse 21 and the reference to His body being offered up.

(3) John 6:4. He knew what He would do. Himself purposing to be the Bread of Life, as He stated on the morrow.

(4) John 11:55, 12:1, 13:1. Now is He offered up, and now does He do that which shows Him to be the Bread of Life indeed. "And when I see the Blood I will pass over you."

But this is not the end of the matter; redemption is the prelude to service, and service is always desired by God in relation to His sanctuary: "Ye also, as living stones, are built up a spiritual House, to be a holy priesthood, to offer up spiritual sacrifices, acceptable to God through Jesus Christ." To fall short of this is to be ignorant of the purposes of God in all God's year. Yet it may be noted that this festival and the next could be kept in the wilderness, whereas others could only be kept in the Land of Promise. Alas, we may feel ourselves to be walking in the wilderness when we ought to be knowing ourselves as seated in the heavenly places in Christ Jesus. Yet it is given even to such to connect the two - Scriptures, "Our passover hath been crucified, even Christ" and, "This do in remembrance of Me" (1 Corinthians 5:7, 11:24). The remembrance of the death of our Lord according to His commands, week by week, is of incalculable benefit to a believer. We need to be like Josiah, and to have hearts that are tender and humble before our God, to find blessing such as he found in keeping the word of God.

CHAPTER FOUR: THE DAYS OF UNLEAVENED BREAD

The day after the Passover, the fifteenth day of the month, was the commencement of the Festival of Unleavened Bread. In reality, there was no discontinuity between the two festivals, for the Passover was to be kept "between the two evenings" (Leviticus 23:5, RV margin). This expression is always found in connection with the keeping of the Passover, and it is also used in connection with the offering of the evening sacrifice (Exodus 29:39, 41; Numbers 28:4,8), the lighting of the lamps (Exodus 30:8) and the giving of the quails (Exodus 16:12).

Gesenius, the eminent lexicographer, quotes three interpretations of the expression:

(1) the time between the setting of the sun and deep twilight;

(2) the time between the commencing of the declining sun and the setting of the sun;

(3) the "evening" before sunset and the "evening" after sunset.

Of these, he says, the first is the best supported, and it appears to be confirmed by Deuteronomy 16:6: "at the going down of the sun." Thus, strictly speaking, the Passover commenced at the very close of the fourteenth day, and continued into the fifteenth day, since the Hebrew day commenced at sunset. Hence the Festival of Unleavened Bread began during the Passover feast, in conformity with Exodus 12:18, where it is stated as beginning at the fourteenth day at even. In fact, all leaven had to be put away before the Passover itself was kept (Exodus 12:15,18). Only one reason is given for this Festival: "It is because of that which the LORD did for me when I came forth out of Egypt " (Exodus 13:8; see also Exodus 12:17, and Deuteronomy 16:3), which I would understand to cover more than the events culminating in the passage of the Red Sea. When this Festival was first ordained (Exodus 12), very little was said by way of explanation, even of a superficial character.

No reference was made, for instance, at this stage to the thrusting out of Egypt, and having to use dough that was unleavened because they could not tarry. This contrasts with the Passover, and compares with the Sabbath. Indeed, there is much to be gained by a detailed comparison between the Sabbath and this Festival. The commandments concerning both are very stringent indeed. There is actually more reiteration (and therefore more emphasis) concerning the commands as to this Festival than there is as to the Passover itself, and the extremely serious nature of it in the estimation of God is evidenced by the command that whosoever should eat at this time of that which was leavened should be cut off from the congregation of Israel. Such a command had been given only once before, when the rite of circumcision was enjoined. Later, when the Law was given, similar warnings were given as to the Passover, the various offerings, the Sabbath, the ointment, fat, blood, etc., but it is certainly remarkable that at this moment the LORD should so emphasise this threat (stated twice, for greater emphasis, in Exodus 12:15 and 19).

Clearly, therefore, this Festival is of such importance that great care is necessary in its interpretation. It must be noted in the first place that the seven days of the feast have a different significance from that of, say, the fourteenth or fifteenth days, in that there are no precise events associated with each of the days, though the next Festival, speaking of the Resurrection of the Lord Jesus Christ, necessarily occurs on one of the days. The only reference we have to events occurring on these seven days has to do with the Israelites, in their ordered ranks, with the Ark of the LORD in their midst, encompassing the city of Jericho. Guidance in interpretation may be sought from the seventh month, on the lines previously suggested. Corresponding to this Festival is the Festival of Tabernacles, which begins on the fifteenth day of the seventh month, and lasts for eight days. This does not commemorate a unique event or a definite act, but has to do with a state of things; it shows us the state resulting from the whole of God's previous workings, from Redemption to the Judgment. It is thus the fullest possible expression of God's purposes.

Taking the hint, we may conclude that the Festival of Unleavened Bread also expresses a state of affairs, the condition resulting from God's dealings with men hitherto, especially as culminating in the Passover. His later acts (e.g. Pentecost) are not brought into this except in an indirect manner, so that we shall expect that the character of this Festival ought to be viewed individually rather than collectively, and that condition rather than position will take the first place. The Passover is fundamental to all other Festivals, but it is specially related to the Festival of Unleavened Bread. When Josiah was bringing order into the Land of Judah, and was about to keep the Passover, we read that "Nevertheless the priests of the high places came not up to the altar of the LORD in Jerusalem, but they did eat unleavened bread among their brethren" (2 Kings 23:9,21).

God will not have men to pick and choose in His word, and we may be sure that whatever men may choose to keep is of no avail if the Blood of Christ is left out of account. When the Lord Jesus was crucified, and was buried, the Festival of Unleavened Bread could only be kept by God Himself, and we may conclude that in some measure at least the Festival speaks of Christ. The absence of leaven, of course, points to the absence of sin, for we all know that leaven is usually a type of sin in the Scriptures, and in this respect the character of the Lord Jesus is beautifully portrayed in the type of the unleavened bread. Without any doubt at all, He had these days in view (see John 6:4) when He said, "I am the Bread of Life: he that cometh to Me shall not hunger." Please read John 6:22-59. They that so eat of the Bread from Heaven receive eternal life, and shall be raised up at the last day. Notice the reiteration (five times) of the phrase "eternal life" (or else "live for ever"), and of the statement, "I will raise him up in the last day" (four times), in this short portion.

The seven days of the Festival, as already noted, include the memorial of the Resurrection of the Lord Jesus Christ, the firstfruits of them that sleep. The absolute certainty of the possession of eternal life, and of the hope of resurrection, should follow on the knowledge of sins passed over and forgiven, and all spiritual life and growth is according to the measure of our feeding thus on the Living Bread. Withal, this Festival is one of the Bread of Affliction (Deuteronomy 16:3). Thrust out of Egypt in haste, the Children of Israel early had to recognise that the world hates that which is not of the world. The world hated One without a cause, for in Him was no leaven of sin, and the world hates those whom He has chosen for His own, and unto whom His Father imputes no sin (John 15:18-25). "Ye are unleavened. For our Passover also hath been sacrificed, even

Christ: wherefore let us keep the feast [Greek, festival], not with the old leaven of malice and wickedness, but with the unleavened bread of sincerity and truth" (1 Corinthians 5:7-8).

Thus this Festival speaks of the character of the Lord in His sinlessness, and of the character that believers should have as they partake of the blessings of eternal life in Christ Jesus, and as they rejoice in the hope that God has set before them. It was symbolic of the changed state of things that the Israelites left the land of Egypt with unleavened dough. The corrupting influences of Egypt were also to be considered as having been left behind, as well as the tyranny and bondage. However little the people realised this in a practical way, it is certain that God so considered them as unleavened, "a new lump" (1 Corinthians 5:7), and it is ever His delight for His children to conform themselves in heart to the status that He gives them. In like manner, we are considered a holy people, and the leaven of sin without and within should find no working in us; it should be purged out, that we may be a new lump, even as we are already accounted unleavened (such is a free interpretation of 1 Corinthians 5:7).

In order to preserve this state, we have been given the remembrance of our Lord Jesus Christ, thereafter to keep a seven days' festival with the unleavened bread of sincerity and truth, as our hearts have been touched by thoughts of Him.

"Oh, wonder to myself I am,

That I can view the dying Lamb,

Can scan the wondrous mystery o'er,

And not be moved to love Him more."

Another clue to the interpretation of this Festival is to be found in Exodus 13:9: "It shall be for a sign unto thee upon thine hand, and for a memorial between thine eyes, that the law of the LORD may be in thy mouth." These words are also applied to the words of the Law in Deuteronomy 6:5-8, 11:13-19. God is never content that a people shall reverence the words only of the Law, for He desires all my heart, and all my soul, and all my might. He would have the words written, not on the doorposts of my house or my gates or my walls, only, but upon my heart. Such writing can be of a more permanent character than was desired by Job (see chapter 19:23-27): "Oh that my words were now written! Oh that they were inscribed in a book! That with an iron pen and lead they were graven in the rock for ever!"

For the writings of the Spirit of God upon hearts of flesh will give results that shall outlast even the rocks, and shall endure when the earth and the heavens flee away from the face of Him that sitteth on the Throne. The truly indelible writings are those that come from the assurance, "But I know that my Redeemer liveth, And that He shall stand up at the last upon the earth." It is this remembrance which is to be associated with the hope of resurrection: "Yet from my flesh I shall see God: Whom I shall see for myself." Such are the thoughts that are brought before us in this Festival. Where they find a place in our hearts, they will be made manifest in our lives, and the law of the LORD will be found in our mouths. "If ye love Me, ye will keep My commandments," said the Lord Jesus. This is the final test as to whether our love is genuine, whether we are indeed feeding on Him, and whether we are indeed keeping festival in sincerity and in truth.

CHAPTER FIVE: THE SHEAF OF FIRSTFRUITS

The outpourings of Job's soul concerning his Redeemer may be linked with the testimony of Paul: "If in this life only we have hoped in Christ, we are of all men most pitiable. But now hath Christ been raised from [among] the dead, the firstfruits of them that are asleep" 1 Corinthians 15:19-20). This reference to firstfruits, coupled with the keeping of the first Festival of Firstfruits on the day after the Sabbath in the week of Unleavened Bread, suffices to focus our thoughts on the Resurrection of our Lord Jesus Christ as foreshadowed in this festival. This festival of the firstfruits, and probably all the later festivals also, could not be kept in the wilderness (Leviticus 23:10-15).

The fruits of the Promised Land, either in the form of the sheaf or the fine flour, were necessary to keep the ordinances. According to Numbers 15:2 it would appear that a burnt offering in the land could not be offered without the appropriate meal offering and drink offering. (It is a point worthy of investigation as to how far the offerings could be offered in the wilderness. Do we not, indeed, tend to give the wilderness too prominent a place in our thoughts of the children of Israel? Most of the law was definitely associated with the land and not with the wilderness).

There are certain details in the relevant portion (Leviticus 23:9-14) which need consideration, and it is very remarkable to me that we are thrown back to Exodus 16 and that thoughts concerning the manna are once more brought before us. In the first place, the word translated "sheaf" is the word omer, which is found to be principally used in Exodus 16 and Leviticus 23. It is presumed that the omer represents the amount of grain that would result. Also notice the last verse of the former chapter, "Now an omer is the tenth part of an ephah." We may be sure that this seemingly irrelevant remark is intended to force our attention to something. Throughout the Old Testament we find a dry measure occurring under the term "a tenth deal" or "a tenth part." In the Revised Version this expression is translated "the tenth part of an ephah," and the words in italics seem to be substantiated, though they do not occur in the original. If this is correct, we have in this portion not only the omer of grain, but two omers of fine flour required for a meal offering.

Further, there is something remarkable about this meal offering. If we turn to Numbers 15:2-12, we shall find the details of the meal offerings and the drink offering associated with three grades of burnt offerings—the bullock, ram, and lamb. The amounts of fine flour and the quantities of wine ordained for each grade are faithfully adhered to throughout the Scriptures (as may be verified by patient use of a concordance), except in the present instance. Whereas normally, for a he-lamb, only one omer of fine flour is used for a meal offering, here two omers are ordained. The amount of fine flour is doubled, but the amount of wine is as usual. These considerations clearly determine the leading thoughts of the LORD concerning the Resurrection of our Lord Jesus Christ. The omer, even allowing for differences in food values, according to Exodus 16:16, represents a man's eating, but the omer of firstfruits clearly must be anticipative, in that the grain has not yet been converted to flour. The normal meal offering is generally understood to typify the life of the Lord Jesus upon earth; that is, it is retrospective. Now He was raised, not only for what he had been, but also for that which he was to be. We see these two points brought before us in this portion, in the sheaf and in the fine flour.

After much consideration, I have concluded that it would be wrong to consider the two omers of fine flour as typifying in themselves the past life and the future life of the Lord, because we are faced with the same facts in connection with each of the two loaves of the next festival. The more logical interpretation would be to consider, not the doubling, nor the fact of two omers, but rather the usual character of a meal offering of this amount. Thus, we have a lamb as a burnt offering, with the meal offering appropriate to a ram. Please read Genesis 22. The "lamb that God provided" proved to be a ram (verses 8 and 13) a difference that is often glossed over. Now read Exodus 29 and Leviticus 8, and it is clear that the ram is used in connection with the consecration of the priests. The fact that in Exodus 29:24 we have the very first reference to a waving of a wave-offering, such as we have in connection with the wave-sheaf in Leviticus 23, testifies very greatly to the validity of this mode of interpretation.

We note that the wave offering of Exodus 29 also includes various grades of meal offerings of unleavened bread (verse 23). Pursuing this thought, we see the Lord Jesus Christ, who had offered Himself, still considered as a burnt offering, typified by the lamb rather than the ram. It is important to notice that the Lord was not made a Priest because of having offered Himself up as a sacrificial ram. He did not so glorify Himself to be made a High Priest, but in the days of His flesh, having been heard for His godly fear, having learned obedience by the things which He suffered, and having been made perfect, He was named of God High Priest after the order of Melchizedek (Hebrews 5:5-10). What we here read is precisely that which is brought before us in a meal offering - the life in the flesh.

In Philippians 2 we have the thought of the Lord in all His humility, a Lamb indeed. As a lamb, He died, but the life that He lived showed Him worthy in the sight of God to be made a Priest for ever, after the order of Melchizedek. In conformity with this view, we have the drink offering appropriate to the lamb. It is significant that in Leviticus 23:10-11, we have priestly work brought before us. We are in no doubt as to whom this speaks of. The Lord Jesus Himself was the one who waved before Jehovah the firstfruits of the harvest. This waving is a beautiful picture of the triumphant appearing of the Lord before the Father. "Touch Me not," He said unto Mary, "for I have not yet ascended unto My Father." Later in the day, He allowed the disciples to handle Him freely. Surely we cannot resist the conclusion that the triumphant One had appeared in glory before the Throne of Jehovah. No human pen can outline for us the majesty of the heavenly scene when the Lord of Glory (1 Corinthians 2:8) entered into that presence. That triumphant entry is faintly pictured for us in Psalm 24:

> "Lift up your heads, O ye gates; Yea, lift them up, ye everlasting doors; And the King of Glory shall come in. Who is this King of Glory? The Lord of Hosts, He is the King of Glory."

The Lord of Hosts indeed! Yet this is the one that is spoken of in that same Psalm, in answer to the question, "Who shall ascend into the Hill of the Lord?" He alone it was that had the clean hands and the pure heart, Who had neither lifted up his soul unto vanity nor sworn deceitfully. It is this One that is to receive "the blessing from the LORD, and righteousness from the God of His salvation." This was the beginning of the joy that was set before Him, that He should be the firstfruits of them that are asleep; Christ the firstfruits then they that are Christ's, at His coming. This is indeed a picture of promised glory and blessing.

When we contemplate the glorious fact that the resurrection of Christ involves that we also, if we fall asleep, shall be raised to eternal glory, and that we are even now enjoined to know ourselves as raised with Christ, we cannot contemplate ourselves as walking in the, wilderness. A believer whose thoughts are taken up with wilderness experiences (and, alas, the wilderness is too frequent a theme) will know little of the joy of the Lord.

CHAPTER SIX: THE FEAST OF WEEKS

After the Feast of the Wave Sheaf there was an interval of 50 days (Leviticus 23:16) and obviously the Feast of Weeks, as it was generally called (Deuteronomy 16:10), has to do with the events of the great day of Pentecost. This interval is further described in the words, "Seven Sabbaths shall there be complete." We have a similar conjunction of terms in the seven Sabbatical Years and the fiftieth year, the Year of Jubilee, and we should therefore anticipate some connection in interpretation. The Year of Jubilee speaks of the consummation of all things, the liberation of captives, the comforting of broken-hearted,, etc., still in the future, but which we anticipate now only because of what took place after Pentecost.

The seven Sabbaths call our attention once more to the fundamental subject of rest, which we ought to keep before our minds throughout these studies. During this period there has been a rest of God indeed, depending upon His appreciation of His Son. Now the darkness of the world is to be illuminated by the Holy Spirit, who descends upon the disciples, indwells them, and consecrates them to the service of God. It was a day of firstfruits indeed. The word used in Leviticus 23:17 differs from that used for the sheaf in verse 10, in that the former is commonly used (with other derivatives from the same root) for firstfruits or firstborn, while the latter implies first in place or time or order, and it is used for the head (literally or figuratively).

Christ is the Firstfruits and believers are a kind of firstfruits (James 1:18), but Romans 8:18-25 widens the view as to firstfruits. It is a glorious fact that God ever looks onward, bestows the earnest upon us and enjoins us to anticipate the complete inheritance; He redeems us and exhorts us to wait for the redemption that shall be. So Peter quoted from Joel on the Day of Pentecost, "I will pour forth of My Spirit upon all flesh," yet we know that we shall see this fulfilled indeed in a day not yet come. The grand thing is that the Spirit is poured on all flesh, that "the creation itself also shall be delivered from the bondage of corruption unto the liberty of the glory of the children of God. And ... ourselves also, which have the firstfruits of the Spirit, even we ourselves groan within ourselves, waiting for ... the redemption of the body." Corresponding to this, we have the two loaves, baked with leaven, brought out of their habitations for firstfruits unto Jehovah.

It is remarkable that special loaves were not to be prepared, and I see a connection with 1 Corinthians 1:26-31. The common things, the base things, the things that are not, has God chosen, that He that glorieth may glory in the Lord. Yes, and the things that could not, by the Law, be offered to God at all are commanded by God as a new meal-offering, for the corrupting leaven (its operation killed by fire) is allowed in the loaves to be waved before God. It was not a new thing for leavened bread to be offered to God, for one of the grades of peace-offerings required leavened as well as unleavened cakes to be offered (Leviticus 7:11-34;), to be waved before God, and this was in connection with the highest grade of peace offering, that for thanksgiving or praise. As we have already noticed, a meal-offering was the almost invariable accompaniment of a burnt offering, which we usually associate with thoughts of praise and the new thing is that a leavened offering could now be offered as a meal-offering.

It is well at this stage to consider what happens to the loaves. Certain burnt offerings are offered with them, along with a he-goat as a sin-offering, and two lambs as a peace-offering. Now the ordinary law of the peace-offering required certain portions to be waved, and certain others to be heaved, for the priest, while the offerer feasted on the rest. In the present instance, we infer from verse 20 that the two leavened loaves are waved with the wave-breast, and that the priest receives these, with the residue of the lambs, for himself. Therefore the two loaves are waved as though they are part of a peace offering for thanksgiving. So far, in God's year, the priest, typically speaking, has had nothing, for all the previous offerings have been burnt-offerings, wholly for God. What then, is there today, or what was there on the day of Pentecost, that we know pertains to Christ? "Ye are Christ's," says Paul (1 Corinthians 3:23), and, if so, "Then are ye Abraham's seed," and as Christ's we are one man in Christ Jesus, and in Christ Jesus there is neither Jew nor Greek (Galatians 3:28-29).

It is not "in Christ" but "in Christ Jesus" that we are now one. Prior to this there was the twain which were created one new man, so making peace. See Ephesians 2:11-17, and note emphasis on peace; then consider the import of the peace-offering of the Feast of Weeks. In John 10:16 we have the Lord speaking of His sheep and the other sheep not of this fold, which shall become one flock with one shepherd. This brings us to that interpretation of the two loaves which regards them as typifying Jew and Gentile. There is no essential difference between the two loaves, just as there is "no distinction" (Acts 11:12) between Jew and Gentile. The usual interpretation of a meal-offering is that of the life of Christ, and now we have brought before us the lives of ordinary men ("out of your habitations"). The leaven in the loaves was there already, and so cannot represent anything resulting from the operation of the grace of God as on the Day of Pentecost. These lives are to be considered as the Lord's, a point which needs emphasising again and again.

In our portion of Leviticus 23 we have a number of twos which need to be connected together in our interpretation. The two lambs offered as a sacrifice of peace-offerings are clearly related to the two loaves, as we have already seen, and the connection suggests thoughts of service in thanksgiving and praise, while the two rams offered as burnt offerings support this view. We suggested in connection with the Wave-sheaf that consecration is brought before our minds in the two-tenth parts of an ephah of fine flour, the offering appropriate to a ram. We have this same quantity in each of the two loaves, and the conclusion is almost irresistible, from the quantities of fine flour, the two rams, and the suggestions as to peace-offerings for thanksgiving, that these things are intended to speak of the lives of people set apart, consecrated, waved before God, for the service of the Priest, our Lord Jesus Christ.

It may be noticed that the burnt-offerings include seven lambs and one bullock, with their meal-offerings. There is also one he-goat for a sin-offering, but there is no trespass-offering. It may also be noted that in Numbers 28 the offerings commanded to the people are always two young bullocks (one in Leviticus), one ram (two in Leviticus), and seven he-lambs (verses 11,19,24,27), during the festivals of the first six months, a change taking place in the seventh month. I cannot give any explanation of the differences between Leviticus and Numbers in this matter, but I have already suggested that what we have in Numbers is for a sin-stained people, while Leviticus 23. gives essential things as God sees them.

Thus there is always a sin-offering in Numbers 28. and 29 for all festivals, but only one is ever noticed in Leviticus 23, and that is on the Day of Pentecost.

The bullock (perhaps because of its value) is generally used by or for the priest or the congregation, whether as burnt offering or as sin-offering, according to the circumstances. The bullock and the ram, as burnt offerings are associated together chiefly in matters of consecration. The absence of a trespass-offering calls for comment. From Leviticus 7 we see that a trespass-offering must be a ram, and there must be restitution plus the addition of a fifth part. The Scripture is wonderfully precise, and two-tenths is not confused with one-fifth, but the relation is suggestive of thought. A trespass is an offence against God, whether He or men have suffered loss, and as such it is an offence against consecration, or sanctification. The ram of consecration is offered once for all as a burnt-offering, but if there is a violation of this state the equivalent ram of the trespass-offering must be offered. In the former case the appropriate meal-offering involves two-tenths deals and in the latter case the restitution involves the added fifth-part.

We see that a trespass-offering could not be considered in this festival because it is not required in the day of consecration. Therefore this omission adds greatly to the arguments I have given for emphasising the aspect of consecration. The seven sabbaths and the seven lambs are obviously related, and they probably speak of that aspect of rest which God has in Christ; the bullock, the rams, and the two loaves, speak of men set apart and consecrated to be priests unto God, to be associated with the place of His rest, to offer sacrifices of thanksgiving as they enjoy peace and rest in Christ. However far men may fall short of this, we must see what God's purposes are. In a coming day all the saved in Christ shall be a people for God's own possession, and for His glory, and this is what God sees on the Day of Pentecost. Happy are they who are seeking the place of God's rest to-day, having their lives, their bodies (in spite of all the sin that so easily besets them) set apart to the service of the Great Priest over God's House.

CHAPTER SEVEN: THE GLEANING OF THE HARVEST

After the Feast of Weeks is over, there is a comparatively long interval to the next festival, and, in fact, there is nothing as yet to correspond to the events foreshadowed by the later feasts. In the meantime, this day of grace, there are events beautifully foreshadowed in the ordinance concerning the gleaning of the harvest, and we need to consider more closely the typical teaching of the harvest.

The two Festivals of Firstfruits are called "The Feast of Harvest," while the next three festivals are collectively called "The Feast of Ingathering," and we see from Leviticus 23:39 that the last festival of all in this latter group is after the gathering of the "fruits, of the land." According to Deuteronomy 16:13 this means gathered in from the threshing floor and from the winepress, while the promise given in Leviticus 26:5 implies that under the most favourable conditions the threshing would last until the vintage, and the vintage until the sowing time; that is, the harvest is over before the vintage begins. We all know what the Lord said about the harvest being plenteous, and how He speaks of the Lord of the harvest (Matthew 7:37-38); it is a harvest of mercy, a harvest to be reaped at the earliest possible moment. How pregnant are the words of the Lord in John 4:35!

Men would consider the harvest as due "four months" hence, but He is wiser, for an over-ripe harvest can give Him little joy. The "harvest of the earth" at the last great reaping (Revelation 14:15) is over-ripe (Greek: dried-up), but it is reaped before the fully-ripe "vintage of the earth" is reaped and cast into the great winepress of the wrath of God. It is a great help to consider these truths as to the harvest and the vintage, for some believers go astray when they accept interpretations of prophecy which suggest a harvest of mercy in any sense synchronously with a vintage of wrath.

We may now turn to Leviticus 23:22 and note the commands of God to the faithful Israelite, remembering that he was obliged to keep those commands, as is generally the case, in ignorance of the things foreshadowed. "When ye reap the harvest of your land" is an expression befitting the corporate acts of the people of God in keeping His festivals, but it goes on to say, "Thou shalt not wholly reap the corners of thy field." Such a command comes home to the individual; he has a definite responsibility laid upon him to remember the merciful character of his God. Moreover, to give added force to the command, there is the solemn statement, "I am the LORD your God," an expression which occurs twice only in the chapter. The reaper of the harvest must give firstfruits and rejoice before the LORD his God (Deuteronomy 16:11-12), and as he contemplates the Giver of All, he is called upon to remember that he was a bondsman in Egypt. Truly, the recollection of mercy received is always a great help in our dealings with others.

Apart from faithfulness in this, the Israelite had no direct benefit from the gleanings, but the work of gleaning, the joy and reward of gleaning, were committed to the poor and to the stranger. The Israelite who had waxed poor was not thereby absolved from the duty of presenting himself before the LORD his God, there to make his offering and to rejoice with the Levite and the widow and the fatherless in the midst of the faithful and prosperous Israelites (Deuteronomy 16:11-15). Even the poor man could not appear empty before the LORD, but had to give as he was able, according to the blessing of the LORD. If that blessing was received through the arduous work of gleaning, it was according to the mercy and grace of God, and none can offer to God save what He has given to them.

God also provided for the stranger, and it is well to note that there are a number of ordinances dealing with strangers, sojourners, and aliens. The word here translated "stranger" is 'geyr', meaning a temporary guest, not necessarily a foreigner at all. Those that were not Israelites by birth are referred to by the word 'nekar', which is derived from the root 'nakar', a primitive root meaning to scrutinise; another derivative is 'nokriy', meaning an alien or foreigner. These latter words are used concerning the alien that must not eat of the passover (Exodus 12:43); Ruth, in speaking of herself to Boaz; and Ittai, the stranger and the exile from his own country (2 Samuel 15:19). Both words are used together by Moses when he says (Exodus 2:22), "I have been a sojourner [geyr] in a strange [nokriy] land." The clear distinction made between the Israelite stranger and the alien stranger is of great importance. In the ordinance concerning the gleaning, the stranger is not an alien, but is one who is called upon, like the poor man, to render unto God and to rejoice with his host in the place where God would meet with them (Deuteronomy 16:11).

I have stressed this point as to the standing and duty of the stranger even though some may be disappointed that the aliens are not more explicitly referred to, for it must be remembered that we are not dealing only with salvation of sinners. What God has joined together, let not man put asunder, and He has undoubtedly joined together gifts and giving, salvation and service. The law would not permit the alien to participate in service, and thus he is not used here in the type. We have seen that the firstfruits of the harvest must be typically interpreted as the redeemed in Christ, more particularly, however, of those gathered in on the Day of Pentecost. In the days of the Apostles the harvest was relatively abundant, but in these later days the salvation of men and women may be more truthfully represented by the gleanings.

The reaping of the sheaves was followed by the picking-up of the handfulls, and now there is the arduous toil, the back-breaking work, of picking up the ears one by one. It is a day of great faith and of great faithfulness. But some may ask, Who are the gleaners if the gleanings represent the redeemed? Clearly, a change of type is involved, yet we have almost the same transition implied in the term "fishers of men"—the fish of today become the fishers of tomorrow. We may permissibly see the principles of God's mercy exemplified towards those who typically were strangers to the covenant, alienated from the commonwealth of Israel, and poor indeed since they had no hope, of whom Ruth is a type.

The beginnings of the harvest were reaped by those who had the prerogative of birth, the faithful Apostles, but we thank God that a place has been given to the poor and the strangers, yes the aliens, in the great work of preaching the Gospel. In this we are seen, not as receiving blessings that are Israel's, not as reaping in Israel's fields, but as receiving blessings and privileges direct from Israel's God, who said, even of the Israelite in the land of promise, "The land is mine; for ye are strangers and sojourners with Me" (Leviticus 25:23). So the work of completing the harvest is going on, one here, one there, being gleaned. Let us take comfort in this view, if the results of our labours are not what we had hoped and prayed for. Alas for those who will maybe cry, like the Israelites of old, "The harvest is past, the summer is ended, and we are not saved" (Jeremiah 8:20).

To sum up, the gleanings bring before us, I take it, the general principles of God's mercy, of which one, but not the only, phase, is to be seen in the salvation of sinners, while another phase is seen in the relationship of the Children of Israel. Similarly, we are not our own, and all that we have is from God, to be administered as stewards who will have to render account. We should find lessons for ourselves as to our responsibility to care for the poor and the stranger. The great love of the early disciples for the poor is very evident, and when Paul and Barnabas were given the right hands of fellowship as regards the Gentiles, the Apostles only enjoined them to remember the poor, "which very thing," says Paul, "I was also zealous to do" (Galatians 2:9-10).

We also have a special example of this same principle, and in some respects a very significant one, when the Gentiles found pleasure in making a contribution for the poor among the saints at Jerusalem. "Yea, it hath been their good pleasure; and their debtors they are. For if the Gentiles have been made partakers of their spiritual things, they owe it to them also to minister unto them in carnal things" (Romans 15:26-27). Analogous principles are beautifully exemplified in 3 John v.5: "Beloved, thou doest a faithful work in whatsoever thou doest toward them that are brethren and strangers withal." And again, in Matthew 25:31-40, we have a totally different dispensational instance of these truths, where the Son of Man identifies Himself with the poverty stricken and the stranger, and the King shall say, "Inasmuch as ye did it unto one of these my brethren, even these least, ye did it unto Me," and we may well take this to heart as summarising the lessons to be learnt from the gleaners.

CHAPTER EIGHT: THE FEAST OF TRUMPETS

The days of grace so beautifully portrayed in the ordinances concerning the gleaners will end when the seventh month is opened by the blowing of trumpets, not simply to announce the opening of another month, for trumpets were to be blown for this purpose month by month (Numbers 10:10), but to call a holy convocation and to herald a day of solemn rest. The three great festivals collectively called "the feast of ingathering" are about to take place and the great purposes of God are to be consummated. Trumpets were commonly used for the calling of the congregation to the door of the tent of meeting (Numbers 10:3), and in general to call people together as in Nehemiah 4:18-20. I shall seek to show that this solemn occasion of the blowing of trumpets has to do with the gathering of people, firstly in connection with the ingathering of Israel back to the Land, and secondly with the upward gathering of the saints to the Lord.

An important connecting link between the ordinances concerning the gleaners and those concerning the Feast of Trumpets is found in Isaiah 27:12-13: "The LORD shall beat off His fruit, from the flood of the River unto the brook of Egypt, and ye shall be gathered one by one, O ye children of Israel. And ... a great trumpet shall be blown; and they shall come which were ready to perish in the land of Assyria, and they that were outcasts in the land of Egypt; and they shall worship the LORD in the holy mountain in Jerusalem." The words "beat off" come from the Hebrew word 'chabat' which is used elsewhere three times only: Deuteronomy 24:20, Ruth 2:17, Judges 6:11. The first two of these are used in close association with gleaning. Again, the word "gather" is from 'laqat', often translated "glean," as in Leviticus 23. The Margin gives "or gleaned" and the context "one by one" implies that kind of gathering which we have in gleaning.

Thus verse 12 of Isaiah 27 refers to a gleaning of the people of Israel, gathered into the Land, not only one by one, but, as the margin puts it, "one to another." Those that are so "added together" (see Acts 2) are to serve the LORD in His own appointed place. I desire at this point to make a remark of considerable importance if we desire to understand the copious prophetical references to the events referred to above. That is, the gleaning of Israel takes place prior to the sounding of the great trumpet, and it is generally placed in as peaceful a setting as the picture of Ruth the gleaner. There is a peaceful gleaning followed by what we may call an enforced ingathering. Such a contrast is indicated in Zechariah 8-10. In the eighth chapter, the LORD will save His people from the east and the west (verse 7), there shall be the seed of peace (verse 12), and men out of all the nations "shall even take hold of the skirt of him that is a Jew, saying, We will go with you, for we have heard that God is with you."

In chapters 9 and 10 we have the bow, the sword, and slingstones, and the gathered ones "pass through the sea of affliction" (10:11). Thus, in the passage quoted from Isaiah, after the great trumpet is blown, it is those that were ready to perish, and outcasts, who are brought by the mighty power of God to the Land. It is not always easy to connect together the prophecies of the Scriptures, so that the reference to gleaning as well as to the great trumpet is very welcome, and gives us assurance in the interpretation that the Feast of Trumpets has to do with a gathering of people. We have another powerful help in being able to connect together Isaiah 27 and Matthew 24:29-31, through the words "a great trumpet" in Isaiah and the words "a great sound of a trumpet" in Matthew, especially as the marginal readings of the latter are "a great trumpet" and "a trumpet of great sound." These are the only occurrences of the expression "a great trumpet."

In Matthew, the elect are "gathered together from one end of the heaven to the other." We notice that this gathering is after the great tribulation (verses 21 and 29), and it is after the Son of Man has appeared (verse 30), and the tribes of the earth have mourned over Him, which latter things are closely connected, as we shall see, with the Day of Atonement on the tenth day of the seventh month. Since the Festival of Trumpets is on the first day of the seventh month, there is thus an apparent discrepancy between Leviticus 23 and Matthew 24. I suggest that the explanation of this is that the great ingathering takes place in three stages:

(1) the gleaning of the willing-hearted prior to the first day of the seventh month;

(2) the beginning of the enforced gathering on the first day of that month (Leviticus 23); and

(3) the completion of the work when the Son of Man comes in His might and glory and sends out His angels (Matthew 24).

We take it that the great tribulation lies typically between the first and tenth days of the seventh month of God's year. The enforced ingathering would thus correspond to the ingathering of the over-ripe harvest of Revelation 14:15. If this be so, then the acts of the seven angels of Revelation 8-11 are to be seen between the first and tenth days—that is, the typical days, for the acts of the seven angels occupy a long period (Revelation 9:5). The Feast of Trumpets, in my judgment, is that which takes place when Jehovah God (Zechariah 9:14) shall blow the trumpet, and there is no event prefigured between the King coming to Jerusalem, riding on the foal of an ass, and the blowing of this trumpet. It is the act of God Himself, and the festival no doubt takes into account the seven trumpets that are to be later blown by the angels. It seems conclusive that it is erroneous to take the seventh trumpet as the one corresponding to the Feast of Trumpets.

Returning to the gleaning of those whom I have called the willing-hearted Israelites, this is a phenomenon that can and does take place in our day of grace. The signs of the times undoubtedly point to the drawing near of the day when the children of Israel will be compelled to return to their ancient home, and to do so in days of affliction {Editor's note: this statement was written in 1938, some 10 years before the state of Israel was established in 1948}. The comments on the gleanings in the last chapter were almost entirely confined to their application to believers in Christ, and we have now applied the Scripture to the Israelites. We need to bear in mind that in the festivals God reveals His purposes not only concerning believers, but also concerning the chosen people of Israel. The latter will have their Mount Zion on earth, but just as surely we shall have the blessings of the heavenly Mount Zion. Our lot will be in heaven, not on earth. If today we have a better covenant and a better High Priest, so in the future we shall have a better Land.

Some have doubted whether there is anything for us in the ordinances concerning the last three festivals, and they would give them an entirely earthly fulfilment for Israel. But if the Sabbath, the Passover, the Resurrection, and Pentecost, have to do with us, it seems logical to conclude that the rest have also a fulfilment for us. There is absolutely nothing in Leviticus 23 to indicate that the redeemed are no longer to be seen in the ordinances concerning God's year. Clearly, therefore, if we can see something for us also in the blessings of the Feast of Tabernacles, we should take to ourselves what is said concerning the Feast of Trumpets and the Day of Atonement, remembering only that our future is in heaven. There is, of course, one great ingathering that we are to look forward to with gladness, when:

> "the Lord Himself shall descend from heaven, with a shout, with the voice of the archangel, and with the trump of God: and the dead in Christ shall rise first: Then we that are alive, that are left, shall together with them be caught up in the clouds, to meet the Lord in the air" (1 Thessalonians 4:16-17).

There is no definite article (the) before either "archangel" or "trump of God." We thus cannot safely compare this trumpet with any other, not even the great trumpet, nor can we readily say what the voice of archangel means; it is probably a great voice (see Revelation 1:10; 5:2; 7:2; 10:3; 11:12; 12:10; 14:7,9,15; 16:1,17; 18:2; 19: 1,17; and 21:3, for examples of great voices). According to 1 Corinthians 15:51-52, "we shall all be changed ... at the last trump: for the trumpet shall sound ... "Here the "last trump" takes the definite article. We conclude that it is not the last of several trumpets (certainly not the last of the seven trumpets of the Revelation), but the last trump of one trumpet, and it is mentioned here because a precise moment of time is referred to—"in a moment, in the twinkling of an eye."

It would thus seem that the trumpet will sound again and again, that trumpet that is associated with the power of God (a trump of God). The glad shout of the Lord, as He descends, will be followed, perhaps, by the great voice giving such a command as we have in Revelation 11:12, or making such an announcement as we find in Revelation 4:1: "Come up hither." The trumpet shall sound, maybe, again and again, while we His people shall turn with glad surprise "to see the voice." Some short interval is thus indicated in which the Lord's presence will be manifested in the air (compare Exodus 19), and we shall listen with eagerness, maybe, to the sound of words and the voice of the trumpet waxing louder and louder, until the last triumphant shout shall sound, and we shall ascend into the air, to meet our Lord, and to be for ever with Him. A Festival of Trumpets this shall be indeed!

Many, no doubt, have become accustomed to the idea that we shall have no precise indication that the Lord is in the air until we find ourselves there with Him. What I have already suggested concerning the shout, the voice, and the trumps, may thus be new to many readers. But consider this—we are not told that it is the coming of the Lord that is in a moment, but it is the raising of the dead and the changing of these bodies that are said to take place in the twinkling of an eye. Moreover, what we call the coming is literally the presence (parousia). I judge, therefore, that not only is there "the seeing of the day drawing nigh" to make us the more expectant, but there will be a short interval between the glad descent of the Lord and the ascent of His people. It was never intended of God that that coming should find us unprepared, whatever may be thus true of the coming of the Son of Man (1 Thessalonians 5:1-6). There may be times and seasons (Acts 1:7, 1 Thessalonians 5:1) concerning the restoration of the kingdom to Israel, and concerning the coming of the Son of Man the hour is known only to the Father (Matthew 24:36), but these are not applicable to us, for we are supposed to be as those that watch.

We ought to take into consideration the significant fact that the earlier festivals have been fulfilled on the appointed days, not only in the general sense of that expression, but literally, according to Leviticus 23. None knew in what year the Lord would become the Passover Lamb, but on the appointed day of the year He died. Then came the waving of the Sheaf of First-fruits on the morrow after the sabbath, followed by the Day of Pentecost, on which day the Holy Spirit descended, and the Spirit's work in this dispensation commenced. If God observed the days of the Festivals at the beginning of the dispensation, may there not be something analogous in this at the close, with reference to the Lord's coming and the Feast of Trumpets? What I have said in the last two paragraphs, if correct, goes a long way towards resolving many difficulties in connection with the coming of the Lord, particularly in connection with the attitude of His people.

How dreadful to think of estranged brethren going together! If they be not agreed, they cannot even walk together. I believe that there is need for very great exercise among God's people regarding this matter, and I also believe that the Scriptures would teach that He will come to a waiting and watching people, in which connection Acts 1:9-11 appeals to me very powerfully. They were looking steadfastly into heaven as He went, and that, I judge, will characterise us in the day of His coming. To be keenly alive to the possibilities of the first day of the seventh month, and the waiting period on that day, would mean an incalculable intensive preparation of heart among the Lord's people. The world in its darkness knows not God, and that darkness will not be dissipated until the Sun of Righteousness arises, though we who are the children of light wait not for that, but for the rising of the Bright, the Morning Star.

Surely that star which is known to us as Venus, and which the ancients called Phosphorus long before the day of Peter, is as a sign set in heaven, as it shines in all its beauty prior to sunrise! "We have the word of prophecy made more sure; whereunto ye do well to take heed, as unto a lamp shining in a dark place, until the day dawn, and the day-star (phosphorus) arise in your hearts" (2 Peter 2:19). Oh, that we could have in our hearts such thoughts concerning the Lord's coming that even now, through faith, the Holy Spirit may so give us a foretaste of the coming joy that we may be ready to cry, "Amen, come, Lord Jesus"!

CHAPTER NINE: THE DAY OF ATONEMENT

The joyous celebration of the Feast of Trumpets is followed by the keeping of the Day of Atonement, and the ordinances concerning this are introduced by the somewhat ominous word, "Howbeit." This is the day of judging, the day of affliction of soul, a very solemn day in Israel's keeping it, and an exceedingly solemn day in the purposes of God. To understand rightly the significance of this solemn day, it is necessary to consider the various references made to it in the Scriptures, with special reference to the parties concerned.

Most of us would immediately think of the striking events recorded in Leviticus 16., when Aaron puts on the holy garments, and presents the blood of the bullock of the sin-offering which is for himself, and casts lots upon the two goats, one for the LORD and one for Azazel. This is the solemn occasion when the High Priest enters into the Holy Place, "once in the year, not without blood, which he offereth for himself, and for the errors of the people" (Hebrews 9:7). This is the day when the iniquities of the people are confessed over the live goat, "even all their sins," and they are put on the head of the goat, to be borne by him unto a solitary land. Now compare Numbers 29:7-11, where many offerings are referred to which are not mentioned in Leviticus 16 and 23, while the various episodes of Leviticus 16 are not mentioned in either of the other places.

The three accounts thus differ as to details, but this difference is explained when we note that the principal part of Leviticus 16 is addressed to Aaron through Moses, while the whole of Numbers 28 and 29 is addressed to the people. The Scriptures thus distinguish between the necessary work of the High Priest, in which the people play only a passive part, and the necessary duty of the people to offer up various offerings because of their condition as an erring people. In Leviticus 23, however, these things are not seen and there are no sin-offerings mentioned at all. As I said at the outset of these studies, we have in this chapter the really essential matters as seen from God's point of view, stripped of all redundancies of carnal things the offering up of which were necessary for men, as for the priest, until a time of reformation.

If we carefully read these three accounts of the Day of Atonement, we shall see that one thing is common to all three—" Ye shall afflict your souls, and shall do no manner of work." Further, this injunction is reiterated very forcibly, even with solemn threats, in the ordinances before us. Thus we have the character of the feast brought out, and it is this aspect that must of necessity engage our attention. The work of the High Priest on this day as kept in the past is full of spiritual instruction in the claims of God upon His people and in the provision that He has made for them, but I shall not enlarge on this as our study is concerned with dispensational truths. I have sometimes wondered, however, whether there will be any antitype of these actions of the High Priest when the Day of Atonement arrives, but we have nothing elsewhere, so far as I know, to throw light on this, and judgment on the matter must be reserved.

Having brought out the fundamental characteristic of the feast, the affliction of souls, we may now seek for such future events as shall have this character, and we shall anticipate an earthly as well as a heavenly fulfilment, the former for the Israelites and the latter for the saints in Christ. There can be little doubt as to the events foreshadowed on the earth. "Behold, He cometh with the clouds, and every eye shall see Him, and they which pierced Him, and all the tribes of the earth shall mourn over Him" (Revelation 1:7). "Then shall appear the sign of the Son of Man in heaven; and then shall all the tribes of the earth mourn, and they shall see the Son of Man coming on the clouds of heaven with power and great glory " (Matthew 24:30). This is the appearing, the epiphany, the manifestation in glory, the revelation of the Lord Jesus, when He comes from heaven, "with the angels of His power, in flaming fire, rendering vengeance to them that know not God, and to them that obey not the gospel" (2 Thessalonians 1:7-8).

We note that the whole earth is concerned in this, and not only the Israelites, for the kings of the earth set themselves in a past day, and the rulers took counsel together, against the LORD, and against His anointed (Psalm 2). At the very moment that He comes the nations will be found gathered together against Jerusalem (Zechariah 12:3 and 14:2) and against the people of God, and there will be such a testing time as happened to Paul, when the Lord of Glory appeared unto him in the way. As for Paul, he "was not disobedient to the heavenly vision," and we may hope that among the tribes of the earth there will be some whose hearts will be turned and their souls will be afflicted, and they too will not be disobedient to the heavenly vision. But the "heathen" will continue to rage, there will be some that will not be wise nor instructed, to serve the Lord with fear and rejoice with trembling. Such will rather perish in the way, as they suffer the vengeance meted out to them that obey not the gospel (Psalm 2 and 2 Thessalonians 1:7-8). The flaming fire of the vengeance of the Son of Man will fall, "cutting off" and "destroying" (Leviticus 23:29-30), until the day when He will set up the Throne of Glory (Matthew 25:31), and bring all men to the bar of His judgment.

Such a sight as will be seen when the Son of Man appears with great glory has never been seen on earth, not even when the "glory of the LORD appeared in the cloud" as He came down to speak about a murmuring people (Exodus 16:10); that glory that abode upon Mount Sinai (Exodus 24:16), of which the appearance was like devouring fire on the top of the mount in the sight of the people—so quickly to be forgotten by them as they lusted after the things to be seen and worshipped. The Book of Numbers has many sad references to the seen glory of the LORD—"those men which have seen My glory ... yet have tempted Me these ten times" (14:22); the glory of the LORD that appeared as Korah assembled the congregation (16:19); the glory that appeared on the tent of meeting as the people sought to slay Moses and Aaron (16:42), and the day of vengeance was put off because of the priestly work of Aaron; the glory that appeared to Moses and Aaron (20:6), yet did not cause Moses to sanctify the LORD in speaking to (instead of striking) the rock.

Will it be the glory of the Lord Jesus that will cause the hearts of men to turn in repentance? Will men still be so minded that even the most glorious manifestation of God is but a ten days' wonder to them? The things written aforetime, which we have just considered, will lead to the conclusion that the day is past when God speaks to men thus, and beats them down by the magnificence of His majesty and power and glory. These things do not touch the consciences of men, nor do they cause the tribes of the earth to mourn. Only one thing will God depend upon to bring men to afflict their souls, and that is the evidence of a pierced Christ. In particular, can we imagine the thoughts and feelings of the Israelites, as they look upon Him whom they pierced? On earth they despised the lowly Nazarene, Jesus the carpenter. Not on such a one had they set their hearts and their desires, but they yearned for a Messiah who would come in kingly pomp and glory, who would restore the kingdom to Israel, who would perform vengeance upon their enemies. So, indeed, the Messiah will come, but the Israelites will have to learn that lesson which we have learnt through grace, that the greatest enemies are within, and that these need to be subdued first. Oh, their blindness as He spoke of the things that come from within, that defile the man: "For out of the heart come forth evil thoughts, murders, adulteries ... false witness, railings" (Matthew 15:18-19), and such things have characterised Israel as a nation.

The glory of the Lord will no more prevail over these than it prevailed over the corresponding thoughts in the heart of Satan. But "they shall see Him whom they pierced"—nothing can touch the hearts of men if this does not, nothing else can bring them down into the dust of affliction, nothing else can cause men to mourn with great bitterness as a man mourns for his only son, nothing other than the revelation of the agonies of Christ upon the Cross can avail men, break down their spirits, and make their hearts like wax in the presence of the Lord. When the Israelites thus see that the crucified Jesus is the Lord of Glory, truly the memory of that stubborn, rebellious, and ignorant condition will cause such an affliction of soul as is portrayed in the feast of the Day of Atonement. Will there be any who will withstand such a sight? "Whatsoever soul it be that shall not be afflicted in that same day, that soul will I cut off from his people" (Leviticus 23:29).

Will any offset their rejection of Christ by the memory of their good works? "Whatsoever soul it be that doeth any manner of work in that same day, that soul will I destroy from among his people" (verse 30). Three times we are told in this short portion that no manner of work shall be done; three times is reference made to affliction of soul—it is to be a sabbath of solemn rest. Many would expect that on the day of atonement there would be prominence given to the sin-offering aspect of the death of Christ, but it is worthy of attention that the ordinance is, "Ye shall offer an offering made by fire." This is the basis of atonement, that One was found who offered up Himself, whose life and thoughts were all for the glory of the Father. It is the exaltation of Christ, the manifest subjection unto Him, which makes the Day of Atonement a festival unto Jehovah, and especially is this the ease in the offering of those sacrifices which consist of "a broken spirit" (Psalm 51). It will be true in full measure in that day, as it is written, "A broken and a contrite heart, O God, Thou wilt not despise."

The heavenly aspect of the Day of Atonement is surely seen in the day of judgment that lies ahead of the saints, after the Rapture, and prior to their entering into the joy of their heavenly inheritance and place of service with Christ. It is the only known event for the saints that can correspond in any sense with the anti-type of the Day of Atonement, and I shall seek to show that the principles of God are the same in the heavenly event as in the earthly one, and that some of the details of the festival emphasise and explain some of the references to the Judgment Seat of Christ. On earth, "they shall look unto Him whom they pierced," and it is this which characterises God's dealings with men on this occasion. The work on the Cross has left enduring marks in the body of the Lord Jesus, marks that shall be used in heaven and on earth to testify against the unbelief and wickedness of men, marks that have been used in the past to bring conviction to the minds and hearts of believers, and shall be so used again when we see the Lord. What a wealth of omission there is in John 20:20!

On that resurrection day, when the Lord appeared in the midst, the disciples were terrified and affrighted (Luke 24:37), until He showed them His hands and His side, and even then they disbelieved, for joy! What emotions must have swept over their souls as they gazed on those wounds and on that face more marred than any man's! What passed through Peter's mind we can only conjecture, but surely his thoughts would trouble him as he remembered the time when the Lord looked at him and he turned aside and wept bitterly. Then Thomas was hard to convince of this great joy, until the Lord came again and touched his heart and broke down his doubting spirit, as He said, "Reach hither thy finger, and see My hands ..." but from this lowly place Thomas was able to reach unsurpassed heights when he answered, "My Lord and my God." These incidents show the influence of a sight of those pierced hands.

Will anything more be needed, do you think, on the day of judgment, when you stand before your Lord? Will it not be an occasion of mourning when every eye shall see Him? Will it not be a case of affliction of soul, in the language of Leviticus 23? Surely that sight will be sufficient to bring us down, as the floodgates of our memories are opened to overwhelm us with thoughts of our disbelief, our errant ways, our unforgiving spirits, our absence of love to one another and to the Lord, and of the things done as well as those left undone. When the Lord thus reveals Himself, the counsels of our hearts will be made manifest to us and the hidden things of darkness will be revealed. The character of the mourning in the Land of Israel is vividly expressed in Zechariah 12 and the similarity of the Lord's dealings with the Israelites and the saints (in that all shall look on Him whom they pierced) allow us to apply similar language to the saints before the Judgment Seat of Christ. "They shall mourn for Him, as one mourneth for his only son, and shall be in bitterness for Him, as one that is in bitterness for his first-born."

Will any say, This is surely exaggeration; such a man as Paul will surely not have such intensive sorrow as this? Listen to what Paul says: "With me it is a very small thing that I should be judged of you ... For I know nothing against myself; yet am I not hereby justified; but He that judgeth me is the Lord" (1 Corinthians 4:3,4). Oh! happy man, not to know anything against himself, but note his words—"Yet am I not hereby justified." Put all that Paul did in the scales with the evidences of the love of Christ for him upon the Cross, and the estimate of Paul as to the result is readily surmised. Zechariah helps to clarify our thoughts. The families of David and Nathan are mentioned, of course typically, for our instruction. There was a day when Nathan, the prophet of God, came to David with a tale of robbery and sin, and silenced David with the words, "Thou art the man."

Yet, typically, David and Nathan are seen mourning alike before the Lord, in great bitterness. There was a day when Levi and Simeon went murdering together, and brought upon themselves their father's censure (Genesis 49). Thus Levi ("joined") was one day joined with Simeon in cruel anger and self-will, but later (typically speaking) he was joined to God in service and received a rich blessing, though there is no record of any blessing accruing to Simeon. Yet here they are prophetically seen, without distinction, mourning apart in great bitterness. Would Nathan remember that he was once used of God, and chosen to reprove the anointed king, the man after God's own heart? "Whatsoever soul it be that doeth any manner of work in that same day, that soul will I destroy from among his people," is the answer from Leviticus 23:30. Note the striking picture of every man mourning apart; yes, even the close intimacy of husband and wife is severed, as each mourns apart. It is all spontaneous, agreeing exactly with the thought of Leviticus 23: "Ye shall afflict your souls." It is not that there is compulsion, or that mourning is enforced after judicial sentence. So, I suggest, shall we be before the Judgment Seat of Christ. It will be sufficient for the hidden things of darkness to be revealed to each in his own soul, and as the counsels of his heart are made manifest to him, nothing more will be needed to cause him to mourn apart and to afflict his soul as he realises that the Lord did die for him and he has not returned that love as he might have done.

There is here no suggestion of having our faults paraded before our fellows, and in my judgment it is wrong to suggest such things in connection with the Judgment Seat of Christ. At the judgment of the Great White Throne the procedure is different, for there the books will be opened, and those judged may be given reasons, and may possibly even question the Judge, "Lord, when did we do these things?", as in the case of the judgment of the living nations. Our judgment is according to the measure of the response of our love to the Lord: the character of it will be the same for each of us, but the intensity of it will vary, for some believers will have more to condemn themselves for than others, though none will be exempt from this self-affliction of soul.

"Then shall each man have his praise from God" (1 Corinthians 4:5.). This comes with startling suddenness after reading of the counsels, of the heart being made manifest. We should have expected "blame" here rather than " praise," but admonition by the Lord in front of others is nowhere mentioned, even in 1 Corinthians 3.—"If any man's work shall be burned, he shall suffer loss." This is a Festival of Jehovah, and the spontaneous abasement before His Son will be followed by His joy in giving the rewards for services that have endured the fire, as we have been found "doing service, as unto the Lord, and not unto men: knowing that whatsoever good thing each one doeth, the same shall he receive again from the Lord" (Ephesians 6:7-8). The ordinances concerning the Day of

Atonement throw little light upon the matter of rewards, but it would not become us to leave the subject without saying a little about them.

The Scriptures earnestly exhort us to be diligent, to run as one running in a race, running with a set mind to win the prize (1 Corinthians 9:24). It is a race that requires the laying aside of every weight, and the sin that so easily besets us, a race to be run with patience (Hebrews 12:1), and to be run lawfully (alas, if that day shall manifest to us that we ran in vain!). If we shall faint and become weary, the Scripture significantly says, "Consider Him." What shall be the prizes? There are some that we cannot all expect to obtain, such as the crown of glory that fadeth not away, which is reserved for faithful overseers (1 Peter 5:2-4). There are different degrees of service, and there appears to be a progression of thought in 1 Corinthians 16:23: "Watch ye; stand fast in the faith; quit yourselves like men; be strong."

It is not given to all to be among the warriors or the leaders. "Be strong" were the words fittingly addressed to Joshua, and they befit leaders today. To stand fast in the faith is what we are all called upon to do in some measure and to be overcomers as we do so, and such are promised the crown of life, which the Lord promised to them that love Him, that endure temptation and are approved (James 1:12). Again, "He that overcometh, I will make him a pillar in the temple of My God ... and I will write upon him ... mine own new Name" (Revelation 3:12), that Name which is above every name, which no one yet knows. Again, the overcomer is promised the hidden manna, and the white stone with a new name written, which no one knows but he that receives it (Revelation 2:17). Can our imaginations encompass the joy of being able to take out throughout eternity this testimony from the Lord, something between Him and the recipient alone?

What name shall we rejoice in, that we would seek to have as ours, summing up the Lord's opinion of us? There are many lovely names in the Scriptures, with all their wealth of meaning. "So run, that ye may attain." Some may not be called upon by stress of circumstances and temptation to shine in standing fast in the faith, but there is one thing that each can do, and that is, to watch. The Apostle Paul was well assured of his hope: "I have finished the course ... Henceforth there is laid up for me the crown of righteousness, which the Lord, the righteous judge, shall give to me at that day: and not only to me, but also to all them that have loved His appearing." The Lord speaks in a very beautiful way in Luke 12:35-40, concerning watching: "Blessed are those servants whom the Lord when he cometh shall find watching: verily I say unto you, that he shall gird himself, and make them sit down to meat, and shall come and serve them." Blessed are those servants. If we cannot apply this portion to ourselves, it does at least show the estimation in which the Lord holds those who "love His Appearing." This phase of loving is not confined, either, to the time of His coming, however valuable that may be, but it is a love that will affect our lives, and be instrumental in bringing forth fruit to His honour and glory, and this is possible to us all.

CHAPTER TEN: THE FEAST OF TABERNACLES

The events following on the Day of Atonement upon the earth are hardly within the scope of our study, and only one reference to them may be detected in the ordinances concerning the last festival. It begins on the fifteenth day of the seventh month, when the fruits of the land have been gathered in (Leviticus 23:39). Something has been said in an earlier chapter about the difference between the gathering in of the harvest and the gathering in of the fruits of the land; it was pointed out that the harvest is over before the vintage begins, and that the former refers to the harvest of mercy, and the latter to the vintage of wrath.

After this time of woe upon the earth consequent upon the coming of the Son of Man there will be ushered in the time of the Millennium, when blessings will be showered upon the House of Israel. We note that during the Millennium the nations that came against Jerusalem (Zechariah 14:16) shall go up from year to year to worship the King, Jehovah of Hosts, and to keep the Feast of Tabernacles. The glory of the LORD will fill His temple (Ezekiel 43:2-5, Haggai 2:7-9, etc.), and this shall be a place of worship and of prayer for all nations. This festival covers a period of seven days, thus indicating an extended period as was remarked concerning the Feast of Unleavened Bread. It has an eighth day associated with it, which seems to have been a day of great solemnity indeed. This is the very last day mentioned in God's year, and we know that in the ages to come we shall be shewn the exceeding riches of His grace, and we shall have joy in the presence of our God.

This eighth day is not a "closing festival" (as the RV margin puts it), for the word translated "solemn assembly" does not imply an end, as it is used in circumstances where the last day of a period is not involved, but it rather implies restraint (a day of restraint, according to Newberry); hence the translation "solemn assembly" expresses the character of the day. The eighth day is a day of beginning of a new service or of a new form of service, as we see from Exodus 22:30, Leviticus 9:1 and Leviticus 14:10. Here, a new thing is involved, a new heaven and a new earth, the tabernacle of God shall be with men, and He shall tabernacle with them (Revelation 21:1-3). It is this that the Feast of Tabernacles speaks of, and it is this beginning of a new thing that the eighth day speaks of. Then He who is the Alpha and the Omega, the beginning and the end, shall say, "I will give unto him that is athirst of the fountain of the water of life freely."

It will be remembered that the Lord went up to the memorial of this feast "not publicly, but as it were in secret" (John 7:10), and in the midst of it He taught in the temple. Then we read (verse 37), how on "the last day, the great day of the feast, Jesus ... cried, saying, If any man thirst let him come unto Me, and drink." We recall too how He thus spoke, and prophesied concerning the rivers of living water. This He did according to the Spirit, because He was not yet glorified. This was by anticipation, and we have just seen how that still in the Glory shall He give the same message. It was a message for that present time in anticipation of the glory. From that day in the future, "His servants shall do Him service, and they shall see His face ... and they shall reign for ever and ever" (Revelation 22:3-5). These things are ours by anticipation now, by the Spirit, just as surely as they were in the case of the Lord Himself. What a blessing it would be to each one of us if we saw all our activities here as shadows and faint copies of that which we shall do in Heaven, our earthly service taking the same character as our heavenly service!

There are several Scriptures which indicate an intimate connection between the feasts of the seventh month and service towards God. Thus it was in the seventh month that the Temple of Solomon was completed and dedicated (2 Chronicles 5:1-3), and the Glory of the LORD filled the House of God. We note that this temple was commenced on the second day of the second month (2 Chronicles 3:2), thus indicating something imperfect. It was also in the seventh month when Joshua and Zerubbabel set up the altar whereon burnt offerings could be offered, after which the remnant kept the Feast of Tabernacles (Ezra 3:1,3,4,6), and began to prepare for the temple to be built. Both these have to do with service in connection with the House of God, and we shall do well to bear this in mind as we proceed.

Perhaps the most important occasion on which this festival was kept is that recorded in Nehemiah 8, when the people came together upon the first day of the seventh month and the law of God was read and expounded to them. They were stilled from weeping, for the day was a holy day, a day of joy unto the LORD, and they were exhorted not to be grieved, for the joy of the LORD was their strength. It is indeed refreshing to notice how ready they were to keep the law in all its items, but we may also note that from the days of Joshua this festival had not been kept according to the ordinance. Is it that the available copies of the Scriptures were incomplete, so that in Ezra 3. they kept the feast "as it is written," but only according to the incompleteness of their knowledge? Have we to conclude that during all these centuries, and under the rule of men esteemed of God, the Law was a book to be lost and lost again? Or is it that the people with Ezra were caused to understand more fully something of God's purposes in these festivals and in the details given in the Law? The last would seem to be the proper explanation.

I have previously remarked in connection with the keeping of the Passover that the Israelites would appear to have been very reluctant to remember the sojourn in Egypt, with all its bondage and degradation, but the ordinances of the festivals frequently command the Israelites to remember what they once were. To recapitulate, concerning the Sabbath, they were told, "Thou shalt remember that thou wast a servant in the land of Egypt" (Deuteronomy 5:15); the ordinances concerning the Passover often refer to it (Deuteronomy 16:1), as also those in connection with the Feast of Weeks (Deuteronomy 16:12), and the gleaning (Deuteronomy 24:22). These are the Festivals that have the most definite practical aspect, and we can understand in some measure that the thoughts of Egypt find little place in the remembrance of the Resurrection of the Lord, the Feast of Trumpets, and the Day of Atonement.

The quotations from Deuteronomy are specially significant as being spoken on the eve of entering the Promised Land. Judging after the manner of men we might have conjectured that after the Judgment Seat of Christ we should have finished completely with these bodies of our humiliation (Philippians 3:21), especially after they have been "conformed to the body of His glory." But such is not the way of God. Please read Ephesians 2, and note how the Apostle traces our histories when we were dead ... and walked ... and lived in the lusts of the flesh; then he breaks off to give that wonderfully eloquent passage beginning,

"But God, being rich in mercy." We are caused to see ourselves lifted higher and higher, with great glory and joy set before us in the exceeding riches of grace. Then the Apostle dramatically begins again, "WHEREFORE, remember, that aforetime ye ... were ... separate ... alienated ... strangers ..."

Surely it will accentuate our joy when we look around in the glory of Heaven and remember what we once were. The result will be, "that working whereby He is able even to subject all things unto Himself" (Philippians 3:21). The glory of Heaven did not lead to subjection in the case of the Satanic host, but a new creation will have the ballast of earthly experiences to ensure a right appreciation of the glory and power of God. The Apostle has this in mind, I judge, when writing to the Ephesians (1:8) concerning the grace made to abound toward us in all "wisdom and prudence," Undoubtedly, too, the things wherein we are able to be well pleasing to our God while we dwell in these bodies will remain to give us eternal joy, these being the things that shall withstand the fire of the day of judgment. We may now read Leviticus 23:39-44 with profit in the light of the above remarks, to note that the principal thing in the feast of Tabernacles is that the people shall dwell in booths "that your generations may know that I made the children of Israel to dwell in booths when I brought them up out of the land of Egypt."

To give greater force to this there is added, "I am Jehovah your God." Herein we seem to have a connection with the "wisdom and prudence" of God concerning ourselves, in leaving us in these bodies with all the evil that the flesh is heir to. I suggest therefore that we must seek to correlate the ordinances concerning the booths with our pilgrimage through this world, giving prominence only to those things which shall endure for ever, the things that we can do in these bodies, we who have been "created ... for good works ... afore prepared that we should walk in them" (Ephesians 2:10).

The prominent place given to the booths in which the children of Israel were to dwell during the keeping of this feast encourages us to try to ascertain what meaning may be attached to the materials used in the construction of the booths. We have noted the special significance of the booths themselves in relation to our sojourn on the earth, but every detail given of God is valuable to us. We note that the booths were composed of (1) the fruit of goodly trees, (2) branches of palm trees, (3) boughs of thick trees, and (4) willows of the brook. It is convenient to deal with these in reverse order. We may also note that in Nehemiah 8 there is no mention of willows and goodly trees, but branches of olive, "wild olive," and myrtle trees are specified as materials for the booths.

Willows of the Brook

The only direct reference to the willows of the brook elsewhere in the Scriptures is in Isaiah 44:3-5: "I will pour water upon him that is thirsty ... and My blessing upon thine offspring: and they shall spring up ... as willows by the watercourses." This Scripture is very remarkable because it suggests a connection of thought between the willows of Leviticus 23 and the words of the Lord in John 7:37, "If any man thirst," those words which were uttered on the great day of the feast. We note once again that the words then uttered by the Lord had application to the time now present as well as that to come. This thirst is not that of which the Lord spoke to the Samaritan woman, but it is a thirsting after the blessings that God alone can give (Psalm 42:1-2, 63:1-3), a thirsting after the knowledge of God as revealed in His Word, like the man of Psalm 1, whose delight is in the law of the LORD. "He shall be like a tree planted by the streams of water, That bringeth forth its fruit in its season, Whose leaf also doth not wither."

True prosperity in this world is given to such as this man, prosperity that is measured in the golden coin of the treasure that is laid up in heaven. Further, the willow is a tree which is very tender, slender, pliable, resilient, and thus it can be easily bent and trained. It is indeed a fitting symbol for a man who meditates in the law day and night, whose heart can be touched, whose conscience is a real instrument in the hand of the Holy Spirit whereby the man is bent to the will of God. How gentle are the ways of God with such an one, as He bends without breaking or bruising! Josiah's heart was tender and he humbled himself before his God when he heard the word of the Law (2 Chronicles 34:27). This is an individual matter, and it behooves each one of us to give the Word of God its proper place in our lives. Thus shall we receive of the refreshing water from God. A man who has grown like a willow tree before God is one who can be trained in the ways of God.

Boughs of Thick Trees

The first impression that one gets from reading about the boughs of thick trees is that something really substantial is implied. This is erroneous. The word "thick" does not mean thick as opposed to thin, but essentially it means "wreathed, intertwined, interlaced." The thick trees are what we would call a "thicket." I suggest that the thicket is a very graphic symbol of unity. The interrelation of the saints, the working-out of the principles of being fellow-members of the Body of Christ, members one of another, having responsibility to help one another, to care for one another, are all matters of great moment. The willows of the brook, I have suggested, refer to individuals, but it is not the desire of God that individuals shall live solitary lives. "Behold, how good and how pleasant it is for brethren to dwell together in unity!" (Psalm 133).

Dwelling together in unity is one of the good works that God has prepared for us. The Lord earnestly desired that His disciples should be one, and there is a responsibility laid upon us while in these bodies to maintain this state. It is a very difficult matter to break a thicket by main force, but it can be broken twig by twig. Alas, how easy it is to break off a twig that is already escaping from being inter-wreathed with others! Satan is ever on the watch to break down this thicket of unity. When we stand in the glory it will surely give us delight to remember that during our earthly pilgrimage we stood fast in the bonds of unity. The blessing that comes to a people maintaining this divine condition is incalculable, for it is a state delightful to God, upon which "the LORD commandeth a blessing."

Branches of Palm Trees

The palm tree bears large leaves shaped like the palms of the hands, whence its name. It is symbolic of spiritual growth: "The righteous shall flourish as the palm tree ... They that are planted in the House of Jehovah shall flourish in the courts of our God. They shall still bring forth fruit in old age" (Psalm 92:12-13). It is also symbolic of victory as in Revelation 7:9, where it is also associated with praise. The triumphal entry of our Lord Jesus into Jerusalem will be remembered as the occasion when the people took branches of palm trees and cried out "Hosanna." The palm tree is used in a very remarkable way in connection with the Temple of Solomon. Please read 1 Kings 6. The walls of the house were carved round about, within and without (verse 29), with carved figures of cherubim and palm trees and open flowers; the doors were similarly carved and were overlaid with gold.

The palm tree is not mentioned at all in connection with the Tabernacle. The association of the cherubim and the palm trees is brought out even more prominently in connection with Ezekiel's Temple. The inside wall of the temple, from the ground unto above the door (Ezekiel 41:18-25), together with the doors of the temple, were carved with cherubim and palm trees (no flowers being mentioned). A palm tree was between cherub and cherub, a cherub and a palm tree, a cherub and a palm tree. Similarly, upon the posts of the gates were palm trees (40:16, 22, 26, 31, 34, 37), and palm trees were on each side of the porch (41:26). Surely this is very remarkable, and merits our close attention. The palm tree, with its leaves spread out like hands, used in this connection, would cause us to consider the following Scriptures (see also Psalm 28:2, 1 Timothy 2:8): "Let my prayer be set forth as incense unto Thee; the lifting up of my hands as the evening sacrifice" (Psalm 141:2). "Lift up your hands to the sanctuary, and bless ye the LORD" (Psalm 134:2).

Take these in association with the quotation given above from Psalm 92, and we see that the palm trees speak of men in association with the House of God. The relation between the cherubim and the palm trees reminds us of a fact too often left out of account, that our service in the House of God today upon the earth has a counterpart in Heaven. The Revelation shows very clearly that the heavenly host have a service of praise to God, and we know that we are come (Hebrews 12) unto Mount Zion ... and to innumerable hosts of angels ... When we stand in the glory, lifting up the song of praise to Him that sits upon the throne, when we join in the service of the heavenly host, we shall be exceedingly glad to remember that even upon the earth we so loved the House of our God that it was a delight to offer service well-pleasing to God, with reverence and awe.

The Fruit of Goodly Trees

The word translated "goodly" (hadar) is elsewhere translated "beauty, comeliness, excellency, glory, honour, majesty." Examples are as follows:

"Thou hast crowned Him with glory and honour."

" Honour and majesty are before Him."

The word means "to swell up " and seems to imply all the alternatives given above. Hence the goodly trees are those that are especially beautiful, comely or majestic; that is, they excel in some one quality. It may be that the goodly trees would include the olive and myrtle trees of Nehemiah 8:15, and also that other tree which is there called the wild olive tree in the RV and the pine tree in the AV— there is a certain amount of doubt as to what tree is actually meant. All we can say is that the compound word literally means an oil-tree (hatsee = a tree, shahmen = oil). Various allied words are used in connection with "fatness, grease, oil, etc.," the root notion in all cases being that of abundance, or superabundance. There is an exuding or overflowing. It is very singular that the word "eight" (it will be remembered that there is an eighth day in this festival) is derived from this same word.

Whatever be the actual tree, we are on safe ground in noting that it is used for the making of the two cherubim, and also the doors, in Solomon's temple. It may be that the wood was exceptionally well suited for carved work, but even so we must attach great significance to its use in the House of God. The myrtle tree is a goodly tree in that it excels in beauty, and the olive tree excels in the production of oil that can be used for the service of God and man (Judges 9:9). So excellent is the olive tree in the service of God that David rejoiced, because, he said, "I am like a green olive tree in the house of God" (Psalm 52:8). It was a vision of two olive trees in the House of God that startled Zechariah.

Thus far we have seen that the teaching of the booths has to do with:

(1) the individual life, as shown in the willows of the brook;

(2) unity as shown in the twigs of the thicket;

(3) service in the House of God as shown by the palm trees.

The progression of thought here manifested would lead us to conclude that the goodly trees would speak in some way of outstanding men, leaders, whose lives of faith yield fruit in our lives, whose service in the House of God yields that which honours God and blesses us. We may well thank God for such as have excelled through the mercy and grace of God, the results of whose labours remain for our benefit. May it be indeed the will of God that He will grant us such in our day whom we may honour and esteem highly for their work's sake. They live not to themselves, but their fruit abides in us to the glory of God. As we consider these things, we thank God that here and now it is possible to be well-pleasing unto Him, from Whom light has shone out of darkness to give the light of the knowledge of the glory of God in the face of Jesus Christ.

We know indeed that we have this treasure in earthen vessels, that the exceeding greatness of the power may be of God. The outward man is decaying, yet it is the desire of God for us that the inward man be renewed day by day, as we appreciate more and more the transforming power of the glory of God. The godly men of old knew this, and had witness borne to their faith. The glory of the LORD appeared to Abram when he was in Ur of the Chaldees, Stephen was under the influence of this glory, the disciples said, "We saw His glory," and the glory that appeared to Paul dimmed his sight to all things here below for ever. So all these were strengthened with power, according to the might of this glory, unto all patience and longsuffering with joy.

Such made it manifest that they were looking for things not seen as yet, and as the inward eye contemplated the majesty and glory of God, and as they reflected that glory, so were they transformed into the same image. These were men of like passions with ourselves. Such we can imitate and we ought to imitate them even as they imitated their Lord. Time is earnest, and the golden opportunities rapidly pass by; eternity will reveal to us the great things that God has done for us in Christ, but our studies will have been in vain if we have not been more and more exercised about the claims of that blessed One. Our citizenship is in heaven, so that we are heavenly men walking this earth in earthly bodies. Just as the Lord was in the form of God yet was found in fashion as a man, so we also should realise that we are found in fashion as men, called upon not to become fashioned according to this world (Romans 12:2), but to recognise that in a coming day the Lord will fashion anew these bodies of our humiliation (Philippians 3:21).

As we remember our heavenly future, as we realise the truth that we shall be conformed to the body of the glory of Christ (Philippians 3:21), so ought we to yearn after the present transforming power of God. It is a transformation according to the power of the glory upon our lives, a transformation which takes place by the renewing of our minds (Romans 12:2) that we may prove here and now what is the good and acceptable and perfect will of God. It calls for the presenting of these bodies as a living sacrifice, holy, well pleasing (RV margin) to God (Romans 12:1). The various festivals of Jehovah which we have considered together, the things that are specially well-pleasing to Him, are bound up with His purposes in Christ and also in us. It is my earnest desire and prayer that the thoughts which are expressed in this book will be used of God in His service, that we may find rest in our souls and rest in service, that we may be waiters and watchers, that we may be diligently striving after the rewards of the Lord, and that the glory may be a present reality to us, transforming us and conforming us, making us desirous of the living waters, the unity of the faith, and the thankfulness of heart whereby we, knit together, may offer up service in the House of God with reverence and awe.

CHAPTER ELEVEN: THE YEAR OF JUBILEE (LEVITICUS 25)

One of the great events associated with the Day of Atonement on the tenth day of the seventh month of God's year was the sending abroad of the loud trumpet throughout the land every fiftieth year (Leviticus 25:9). What has been put before us concerning the Day of Atonement in its future fulfilment should help us to understand the significance to be attached to the ordinances concerning the Year of Jubilee then inaugurated. Whatever value this year may have had in the past history of Israel, it can hardly be questioned that its deep abiding value is in that which yet shall be. It is all the more significant to notice that the last three Festivals of Jehovah are festivals of solemn rest, sabbaths in all that is therein implied, and that the Year of Jubilee is closely associated with the Divine thoughts expressed in the Sabbath.

A whole year was to be devoted every seventh year; sabbath rest for the land in which they dwelt should have been a most impressive sign to the people of God that His ways are not man's ways. Further, when the seventh sabbath year (the 49th year in the cycle) was followed by a further sabbath year, the Year of Jubilee, it ought to have increased and strengthened the faith of God's people. Doubters of God's providence and power have always existed, and God dealt with such in all patience: "If ye shall say, what shall we eat the seventh year? ... Then I will command My blessing upon you in the sixth year, and it shall bring forth fruit for the three years" (verses 20-21). Thus did God do also in connection with the manna, in providing for the needs of His people, that His ordinances should not cause hardship but bring blessing to the soul. Though God, for His own purposes, could bring about such a miracle as this, yet He is sparing of His power in matters where men have their own responsibilities.

What God gave to the Israelites was the Land of Promise, to each man a portion which in the grace of God he could call his own, but concerning which he was always liable to be asked, "What hast thou that thou didst not receive?" That which God called "your land" in verse 9, He calls His in verse 23, given indeed (verse 2), and "the land of your possession" (verse 24), but nevertheless subject to the Giver. God's gift was for ever, not to be revoked, but to be used and enjoyed. But man, as a responsible being, is often careless of the gift given unto him, and we read of one that waxed poor (verse 25), with none to help, and he sells the land of his possession—but not for ever! No, says the LORD, it cannot be "sold in perpetuity, for the land is Mine." Hence it is only the right of usage, of tillage, sowing and reaping that can be sold. If a man sell, he is compelled to recollect that there is a day of restoration, that it is only for a certain number of years the "land" can be sold (verses 14-16).

The day came in the land when the loud trumpet proclaimed liberty and restoration to the poor, each man to his own possession, with opportunity now to remember the goodness and the grace of God. In a day to come Israel as a nation will be restored to that which is theirs forever though they have bartered away the fruits of it; through long centuries they have been withheld from the land of their possession, but the day will come when the loud trumpet shall sound—Messiah shall come to earth to restore and to rule. Then shall each man be restored to his inheritance, once more to enjoy the beauteous fruits of the Giver thereof. Surely there are suggestions here for believers in this dispensation. We are not our own, yet God has given to us a gift better far than that of land, a gift pertaining to a new creation, a new life to be lived, to be cultivated and enjoyed, an eternal life with sowing and reaping. Yet this is placed in our responsibility.

Some shall continue to enjoy the fruits of their labours and at the Judgment Seat of Christ will have a rich reward—others, alas, will have nothing! No fruit, no joy, but as those saved by fire—such will be their lot. It is as easy for a believer today to wax poor in spiritual matters as it was for the Israelite of old in material things, for such to barter away the fruits of his inheritance. We may thank God that according to His grace the life cannot be lost. Well it is for us if we estimate the value of our possession according to the multitude of the years or the fewness of the years to that great day of judgment, that we may number our days and get us hearts of wisdom. There is, however, one ordinance of very great interest in connection with this subject, and that is in association with the houses of a walled city, for an exception is here made to the general ordinances, and we stop to enquire why.

It is a very remarkable thing that the great purposes of God are associated with a city. The great men of old desired a better country, that is, a heavenly, and made it manifest that they were seeking after a country of their own, and God was not ashamed of them, to be called their God, for He has prepared for them —a city (Hebrews 11:13-16). We also are regarded as having come to "the city of the living God, the heavenly Jerusalem" (Hebrews 12:22.). We may readily conclude, therefore, that the ordinances concerning the houses of a walled city are related to the desires of God, and we may conclude that these ordinances would have special reference to the earthly type of the heavenly city—Jerusalem. Now we note that it is essential that the city shall have a wall round it, and so great an importance is attached to this that it is stated (verse 31) that the villages which have no wall round about them shall be reckoned with the fields of the country.

It was the desire of a repentant David, again possessed of the joy of his salvation, ready to teach transgressors and to convert sinners, ready to show forth the praises of God, that God should build the walls of Jerusalem. This was a necessary thing before the LORD could delight in sacrifices and burnt offerings (Psalm 51). Again, Nehemiah was greatly grieved when he learnt that the wall of Jerusalem was broken down and the gates thereof burned with fire. Men may come together in their villages and assemblies, from which men may go out and into which men may come at their own will, but God makes no special provision for such. He counts them with the fields; that is, He does not regard them as being anything for Himself in a collective way, and in the spiritual analogy the assemblies of men, believers, which exist to-day without a within and a without, for which there is no wall of separation, are decidedly outside many ordinances of God.

Of such, we may well think of Proverbs 25:28: "He whose spirit is without restraint is like a city that is broken down and hath no wall." This thing in ruins, without provision for rule and government, is but a thing of men whose spirits are without restraint. The LORD loves the gates of Zion more than all the dwellings of Jacob. These words from Psalm 87 indicate the mind of God, for "the dwellings of Jacob" impress upon us that God is not referring thus to a chosen, a called, people. It is sufficient perhaps to note in passing that God speaks of Jacob and of Israel in different senses—the one when referring to individuals and the other when referring to a community. The gates are associated, of course, with the walls. In them sat the rulers of the city, the elders; the gates were the place of judgment, a place where watch could be kept upon those coming in and those going out. Within is an ordered life, there is rule, and, above all, in the city of Jerusalem was the House of God. Little wonder that the faithful Israelites coming up three times a year should rejoice!

"Our feet are standing within thy gates, O Jerusalem ... Peace be within thy walls" (Psalm 122) Such an one, reviewing his lot, might well ponder the possibility of finding a permanent place within those walls, for his own sake and that of his children, of whom it could be true, "The LORD shall count, when He writeth up the peoples, this one was born there" (Psalm 87). Yes, it is still true that God, in the day of judgment, shall place to our account that we loved the place of the Name and desired to be found there, "to dwell in the House of the LORD." Such a one could purchase a house, or probably the land and build thereon within the walls, and it could be his for ever. What a happy privilege to have such a possession! But alas, the hearts of men can become cold even in such a happy condition; that which they once valued they no longer cherish, and they depart, they give up the place. What provision does God make for such?

For one year the Israelite of old had opportunity to repent of his act and to regain his place of residence once more within the walls of the city, but only one year was allowed, and if he failed to find repentance, then the Year of Jubilee did not restore his possession. "Buy the truth and sell it not," says the proverb (23:23). Buyers are often well-spoken of in Scripture. Esau was a seller, and found no place of repentance, though he sought it diligently with tears. These Scriptures in Leviticus 25 illustrate the truths found elsewhere that there is a marked difference between the unconditional gifts of eternal life and the conditional gift of service. Thus the Epistle to the Hebrews has to do with service and place in the House of God; it is a conditional thing—"Whose House are we, if we hold fast" (3:6). From it some may fall away (chapter 6), and some may fall short (14:15), but the eternal life is not in question.

Thus we see that this great Year of Jubilee pictures for us that which will begin when the day of judgment is past, when there will be restoration of joy, but we are called upon very solemnly to consider that our service in the House of God will only be considered as we have been found holding fast to the truth. Alas for those who have given up their place and their privilege and are despising the days of grace given to them in which to repent and find their place back again! This is a joy to be captured here, to be held fast here, and one that will not be restored in the day of judgment. As for us, may the words of Psalm 48 find an echo in our hearts: "Walk about Zion, and go round about her: tell the towers thereof that ye may tell it to the generations following. For this God is our God for ever and ever."

BOOK THREE - LESSONS FROM PRAYER UNDER THE OLD COVENANT

ONE: SOME PRINCIPLES OF PRAYER

The communications of men with God, as recorded in the Old Testament, are not in every case properly to be regarded as prayers in the usual sense of the word. For instance, the replies of men, when God has spoken, are not called prayers; a vow, which implies a voluntary promise to God, is essentially quite distinct from a prayer, which normally and conversely seeks as its object some benefit from God. In these studies, therefore, we shall not consider either the answers or the vows of men Godward, but we shall rather consider those instances in which men have voluntarily cried out to God.

Again, a very large number of occurrences of the word "pray" are obviously only variations of expressions like "Oh," "Oh now," being in fact derived from a word implying incitement and entreaty. For instance, in Genesis 32:29 we have a request in the words, "Tell me, I pray thee, thy name." It is an expression of entreaty, akin to the use of the word "please." Something much deeper and of more moment is implied in true prayer. It is remarkable that we have very little record of prayers in the early part of the Scriptures, but though the word "prayer" is used for the first time in connection with the dedication of Solomon's temple, it occurs in the Psalms somewhat frequently, and also in the Book of Job.

Explicit references to the act of praying are not found until Genesis 20 in connection with Abraham. We are told, however, that men began "to call upon the name of the LORD" in the days of Adam's grandson, Enosh, the son of Seth. The Hebrew word (qara) here translated "call" is used in a wide variety of applications, and it properly means to call out, to address by name. This expression is very frequently used in the Old Testament, in the Psalms as well as elsewhere. Some distinction may be made between this act and that which is more specifically called praying, and it may be well to examine this distinction, and to consider the general teaching of the Old Testament on this subject before proceeding to discuss particular examples of prayer.

It is undoubtedly very significant that calling upon God is first associated with a man whose name means "mortal, frail, or feeble." It is the realisation of impotence which normally leads men in all ages and climes and circumstances to call upon God. Such circumstances are graphically described in Psalm 107. This Psalm of weakness describes those that wandered in a desert way until their soul fainted in them. "Then they cried unto the LORD in their trouble." Others that sat in darkness and in the shadow of death, rebelling, and contemning the counsel of the Most High, were brought very low, and they also cried unto the LORD in their trouble. Fools likewise, as they draw near to the gates of death, cry unto the LORD in their trouble. Lastly, those who have gone down to the sea in ships, and have seen the works and wonders of the LORD in the deep, are constrained, when they are at their wits' end because of the stormy wind, also to cry out to the LORD in their trouble. We note the recurring words, " They cried unto the LORD in their trouble."

Alas! Too often such prayers are but the last resort of men who have been unconcerned about the remembrance of the One whose goodness to the children of men is beyond all our estimation. There can be little doubt that one of the blessings of difficulties is to render us more desirous of the resources of prayer. One has well said, "He that will learn to pray, let him go to sea." Jonah had a similar experience, when he found that he could not escape from having to do with God: "When my soul fainted within me, I remembered the LORD, And my prayer came in unto Thee, into Thine holy temple." (Jonah 2:7). There is this difference, however, between the cries unto God of Psalm 107. and that made unto God by Jonah—the former may have been relatively inarticulate, the mere crying out for aid to the Omnipotent, but Jonah prays. By this we mean that the word used in connection with Jonah is not the word 'qara' but the word normally translated pray. It is the Hebrew word 'tephillah' which is uniformly translated " prayer" in the Old Testament, and its forceful meaning can be ascertained from the root word 'palal', which primarily means " to judge."

In fact this word and its derivatives are used of men acting in judgment, so that the implication is that an active and ordered effort of mind is made towards discernment of persons and circumstances. There is something more in this than in "calling" upon God, though even the latter necessarily predicates that "he that cometh to God must believe that He is, and that He is a rewarder of them that seek after Him" (Hebrews 11:6). Solomon well puts one aspect of this in Ecclesiastes 5:2: "Be not rash with thy mouth, and let not thine heart be hasty to utter anything before God; for God is in heaven, and thou upon earth: therefore let thy words be few." The words of the Lord in Matthew 6:7, concerning vain repetitions, are of similar import. His own example of prayer is a prayer of understanding of the character of the Holy Father and of His purposes, as well as of the needs of the suppliant. True prayer implies discernment, judgment, and understanding. The Psalmist said, "Sing ye praises with understanding" (Psalm 47:7), and much the same thought could be expressed about prayer. In each instance, the thought of being in the presence of a Holy God is such that the understanding man comes with reverence to commune with God, and in his asking he judges himself according to his condition and need, while at the same time he tries to discern the character of God and His desires toward him.

We shall see in due course that it is possible to offer prayer unacceptably to God, and where this occurs it is because of the lack of discernment. This may be so without one being in the gross condition referred to by James (4:1-3), leading him to say, "Ye ask, and receive not, because ye ask amiss." The Apostle John also says, "This is the boldness which we have toward him, that, if we ask anything according to His will, He heareth us; and ... we know that we have the petitions which we have asked of Him" (1 John 5:14-15). Again, this discernment which is indicated as being characteristic of true prayer is not by any means limited in scope; the character of a Holy God is not only to be discerned, but there is a solemn necessity to turn one's thoughts to one's own personal defects and short-comings, even to cry, "Woe is me! For I am undone; because I am a man of unclean lips" (Isaiah 6:5).

Surely the very thought of entering the presence of God should constrain the suppliant to remember his need of cleansing. "If we say that we have no sin, we deceive ourselves, and the truth is not in us. If we confess our sins, He is faithful and righteous to forgive us our sins, and to cleanse us from all unrighteousness"

(1 John 1:8-9)." The supplication of a righteous man availeth much in its working" (James 5:16), is a Scripture which has a measure of bearing upon this matter, for we cannot but think that confession of unworthiness before God, with a calling to remembrance of the precious atoning and propitiatory work of the Lord Jesus, is such that it forms a basis of righteousness upon which God will graciously act to answer our supplications with power from on high.

There is hardly anything so beneficial as self-examination prior to prayer, and one often feels that too frequently assembly prayers lack this prior exercise. Self-examination always leads to the realisation of oneself as being very weak and frail, Enosh-like indeed, and confession is the natural outcome. The thought of having put matters right with God deepens our appreciation of the exercise in which we are engaged, and renders us the fitter for the offering up of prayer on behalf of others. Too often we rush into prayer on behalf of others and on behalf of the work of God without this wholesome self-examination having been made. As one has well said, "Before we pray for others, we should first pray for ourselves."

The above remarks are based upon the root-meaning of the word translated "pray," in the Old Testament. But it is worthy of note that in the passages where the more general word "call" is used we have something to the same effect. In general, we are not given any details of such "calling upon God," but we read in Psalm 99:6-8 concerning Moses and Aaron and Samuel, "among them that called upon His name," "Thou answeredst them, O LORD our God: Thou wast a God that forgavest them." Surely here we have the thought that this calling upon God involved a recognition of the need for forgiveness. The words of Psalm 145:17-19 should be noted. The Lord is indeed righteous in all His ways, and His graciousness a theme of joy. His ear is open to the cries of all men, and He is nigh unto them that call upon Him, provided that such calling is "in truth"; that is, in full assurance and faith and set purpose, reminding us of James 1:6: "Let him ask in faith, nothing doubting."

But let it be noted that the only promise here given concerning fulfilment of desires is unto those who fear Him, which lesson we do well to note. A very important subject is opened up in Psalm 116:17-18 concerning this calling upon God: "I will offer Thee the sacrifice of thanksgiving, and will call upon the name of the LORD. I will pay my vows unto the LORD." Let us notice the divine order. It begins with the sacrifice of thanksgiving and ends with the offering of vows. The variation found in verses 13-14 of the same Psalm is interesting, because the only change is to replace the words "the sacrifice of thanksgiving" by the words "the cup of salvation": "I will take the cup of salvation, and will call upon the name of the LORD. I will pay my vows unto the LORD." The whole Psalm is very lovely in its recollection of the benefits received from God, including that of having been heard aforetime, causing the writer to declaim his love for the LORD (verse 1).

He then asks (verse 12), "What shall I render unto the LORD?" and goes on to speak of the cup of salvation. In Psalm 23 we have the overflowing cup filled up with the benefits of the LORD, and in Psalm 16:5 the cup is associated with the inheritance in Jehovah. There is thus a very close connection between the receiving of this cup and the drinking therefrom in the presence of the LORD, so offering up a sacrifice of thanksgiving. Another variation of these words is found in Psalm 50:14-15: "Offer unto God the sacrifice of thanksgiving; and pay thy vows unto the Most High: and call upon Me in the day of trouble; I will deliver thee, and thou shalt glorify Me." Let it be noted that there is a measure of reproof to Israel in this Psalm, as the Creator testifies His independence of the material offerings of the people, and He goes on to demand the offering up of the sacrifice of thanksgiving and the rendering up of the vows promised aforetime as preliminaries to any efficacious call upon God.

We need to remember indeed that there are certain things proper to prayer, and it behooves us to read the last two verses of Psalm 50: "Now consider this, ye that forget God, ... Whoso offereth the sacrifice of thanksgiving glorifieth Me." We see, therefore, that the teaching of these Scriptures is that the offering up of thanksgiving has a very early place in our approach to God, and that calling upon Him for any matter should follow this sacrifice. The apostolic commentary on all this is tersely put in Philippians 4:6: "In everything, by prayer and supplication with thanksgiving, let your requests be made known unto God." In like manner, we see that thankfulness is conditional also to the offering up of service well-pleasing unto God (Hebrews 12:28, RV margin).

UNDER THE OLD COVENANT

In our studies of prayer in the Old Testament we shall seek to examine the importance of these fundamental conditions of prayer: judgment, discernment, self-examination, confession and thanks-giving.

TWO: THE PRAYERS OF ABRAHAM

We have stated in the first chapter that though men began to call upon the Name of the LORD in the days of Enosh, the son of Seth, yet there is no record of the details of such calling, nor are any prayers referred to until we come to Abraham in Genesis 20. We might note in passing, however, that Abraham refers to a vow unto God in his reply to the King of Sodom, after the slaughter of the kings confederate with Chedorlaomer (Genesis 14:22-24). No other details of the intercourse on this occasion between God and Abraham are given, and as a vow is not in any sense a prayer we shall pass on, after noting that the teaching of Psalm 116 was shown in the last chapter to indicate that the divine order is thanksgiving, calling, or vowing.

When we come to the next chapter of Genesis (15) we have the covenant. Seeing that God speaks first we can hardly consider Abraham's reply as a prayer. Rather do we regard a prayer as that which is offered up to God by one drawing near for this purpose. The same remarks will apply to Abraham's reply concerning the promised son, when he asked that Ishmael might live before God (Genesis 17:18). Though the word prayer is not mentioned in the incidents of Genesis 18, in which God communes with Abraham concerning Sodom, yet in some respect we have reason for considering the words of Abraham as a prayer. We notice in verse 23 that God had apparently finished speaking when Abraham "drew near"—a voluntary act—to speak to God. If judgment or discernment be a characteristic feature of prayer, as we sought to show in the previous chapter, then we see much evidence of this characteristic in Abraham's words, and this is particularly manifested in connection with the attributes of God: "Shall not the Judge of all the earth do right?"

In these few words Abraham reveals a very clear and pregnant knowledge of the righteous character of God, and of His function as the Judge of all. He supplicates God on the basis of what God is, a feature of prayer concerning which we shall have more instances in these studies. It must be truly refreshing to God to find men discerning His character and dealing with Him on that high plane. The expression "the Judge of all the earth" also happily brings Abraham into his proper relation to the LORD, the creature before the Creator, the fallible before the Infallible. There is no confession of personal sin here, such as we have in other prayers, but under the circumstances it would hardly be expected, in view of the manifestation of God's approval of Abraham in verse 17. Nor indeed do we seek to teach that there must be confession of personal sin, for clearly the essential thing is that man must know himself in all his weakness and frailty before God, of which sin is only a symptom.

We do see, however, that Abraham recognises himself in his true position before God, as we have just noted, and very specially in this case when he speaks of himself as "but dust and ashes." Could words be more pregnant than these in this connection? The humility of the man is very engaging, and so is his boldness. It is given unto us to come boldly in the righteousness of Christ, yet it is always becoming to us to do so with reverence and awe. It is very instructive also to notice the balance of persistence and of wisdom. It is sometimes said that God ceased to grant when Abraham ceased to ask. Abraham's boldness increased with his asking, firstly by fives and then by tens. It is at his last request that he excuses himself once more (verse 32), deprecating the anger of Jehovah by saying "yet but this once," and it is probable that he had received some inkling that more would not be according to God's will. It is needful, if we are to be bold, to be also wise, for all the requests made to God are granted only "according to His will."

The expression in verse 33, "The LORD went His way as soon as He had left communing with Abraham," is very interesting. We cannot but think that Abraham, by his persistence and boldness, obtained a knowledge of the ways of God which otherwise would not have accrued to him. The very purpose of God, in knowing Abraham, according to verse 19, was that he might command his children and household to keep the way of the LORD, to do justice and judgment. In this communing with Abraham the balance of justice and judgment is very finely kept. Do not we also find oft-times that in our prayers to God we have our minds awakened in greater measure to the character of God and to His ways? If our minds are exercised in such things in our prayers, if we seek to be discerning men, then we reap the fruit of it through our communing with God in the further strengthening of ourselves in these things. As the use of the muscles in exercise promotes their further use, one of the essential things in physical growth, so also is the case in spiritual growth in prayer. That Abraham was a man of prayer and esteemed by God as such is very strikingly shown in Genesis 20.

The dealings of God with Abimelech in the matter of taking Abraham's wife are in themselves interesting, especially in the way in which God reveals to Abimelech the wrong that has been done. The reply of Abimelech, of course, is not, in our sense of the word, a prayer. Though Abimelech professed to be a righteous man (verse 4), and in fact had not consummated his wrong-doing in actually taking away Sarah, so much so that his integrity of heart (verse 6) is admitted by God, two things alone could save him from death, with all his household—the restoration of Sarah, and prayer. It seems very remarkable that God should give Abimelech this ultimatum in view of what has been said, the more so in that God admits that He has withheld Abimelech from sinning against Himself. If it had only been the saving of Sarah, in view of the birth of Isaac, one feels that God could have used His power to prevent Sarah being taken away at all.

It would almost appear as though God had intended to magnify Abraham in the sight of Abimelech, seeing that it is the prayer of Abraham that is stated as being necessary for the salvation of Abimelech, but, no doubt, there were lessons for Abraham to learn, not to be slow in appealing to God, and the incident may be one of those intended for the learning of those who came after him. We see how efficacious the prayer of Abraham was, in the results to the womenfolk of Abimelech's household (verse 18), but we are not told what Abraham said; the prayer is not related, which means that we are given the kingly task of searching out the matter. This is the first instance in the Scriptures where the word "pray" is used (verses 7 and 17), in the proper sense of the word (tephillah). The greatest point of interest, however, is the role which God gives to Abraham: "For he is a prophet, and he shall pray for thee." This is also the first time that the title "prophet" is used in the Old Testament, and indeed the act of prophesying is not spoken of prior to this. (Of course we realise that Abraham was not the first to prophesy, for Jude tells us of the prophesying of Enoch).

This first reference to both words is therefore of very great intrinsic value, and points us to something of great importance. We could have understood quite readily that the prayers of Abraham on behalf of Abimelech would be of more value than the prayers of Abimelech for himself, in view of the Scripture: "The supplication of a righteous man availeth much in its working" (James 5:16). Prayers on behalf of others are highly esteemed of God, thought for the needs of others being one of His great attributes, and we shall see this in many cases (see also James 5:14-16), but this is very specially the case where the men who so pray are righteous before God, not only judicially so, but experimentally so through confession and prayer on their own behalf. Just as the priest offered for himself first, and then for the people, so it is of prayer, and we have no doubt that Abraham was himself in this ripe condition before God.

But why is Abraham in this place uniquely called a prophet, especially before Abimelech? No doubt God intended to show His choice of Abraham, but there is more in it than that. Abraham was a righteous man; he was prospered of God in material things simply because of the prosperity of his soul (3 John 2), but his great riches lay in the unseen things. To him, God was no stranger-God, but a real presence with him in the pathway of the stranger and the pilgrim; for him there was no abiding city here, but he looked (i.e. waited) for the city that was to come. We read of him that he rejoiced to see the day of the Lord Jesus Christ. It is the working of the Spirit which alone makes these things so real and vital and so leads to the exercise of that spiritual activity which is called prophesying. Within the heart of Abraham was an inward ministry of comfort, consolation, and edification, which is prophesying in its highest sense (1 Corinthians 14:3). There is a reciprocal relation between one's thoughts about these things prior to prayer and one's thoughts during prayer—the one strengthens the other.

It is in and through prayer that we realise that we are in the presence of One who delights to be "the Father of all mercies, and God of all comfort," whose comfort flows to us that "we may be able to comfort them that are in any affliction, through the comfort wherewith we ourselves are comforted of God" (2 Corinthians 1:3-4). Hence, prophesying rightly begins with one's own soul, and renders us more efficacious when we seek to minister to and to pray on behalf of others, as Abraham was called upon to do. The Apostle Paul brings this out in a practical way in Philippians 2.1-2: "If there is therefore any comfort in Christ, if any consolation of love, if any fellowship of the Spirit [i.e., edifying] ... fulfil ye my joy ..." Abraham had not the audience of Isaiah the prophet, but true prophesying, like all things for God, should begin with oneself.

The delight of the inward man in the things which are not seen is something which is well-pleasing to God. The contemplation of the comfort which is in God, and of the consolation which is from God, and of the edification which is by God, has a profound influence upon the soul. It makes the believer to feel what he is supposed to be—a heavenly man inhabitating a temporal body, and yet having a citizenship which is in heaven. To be this in deepest thought and feeling is to intensify every desire of goodness and every work of faith, and makes the approach to God a very real thing. There are obviously many degrees of attainment in prayer, and we must expect to find examples where the spiritual understanding is of lower grade than in other cases. The prayer offered up by Eliezer when on his mission to seek a wife for Isaac is clearly not on the same level as those of Abraham, as we may see after reading Genesis 24:12-14. We notice the diffidence of Eliezer, how he comes, not unto his God, but unto the God of his master Abraham. He pleads that kindness might be shown unto his master; it is for his master's sake that he draws near, and partly too for his own that his perplexities might be resolved by a sign.

We see none of the marks that we have indicated as characterising prayer in its fullest sense—neither discernment, nor confession, nor thanksgiving. The word "pray" in Genesis 24:12 is the elementary term of entreaty which is often translated "Oh now," akin, we said, to the word "please," so that we must not build on this word itself more than we ought in our study of prayer. Nevertheless, we gladly recognise the grace of God in that His ear is open to the most elementary of requests, and we trust that our remarks will not be found deprecatory of the simple requests which the youngest and least instructed of us is encouraged to offer, but rather that we may seek to discern such principles as will be beneficial to us in our learning to pray. In this we learn by example, as well as by contrast and by comparison. We have no record of any utterance by Isaac to God, not even when God spoke unto him at Beer-Sheba, but we do read that on that occasion "he builded an altar, and he called upon the name of the LORD" (Genesis 26:24-25). The blessings he bestows upon his sons can hardly be called prayers, seeing that they are not addressed to God.

THREE: THE PRAYERS OF JACOB

The record of the intercourse between God and Jacob commences when God speaks to Jacob in a dream, leading him to set up as a pillar the stone which he had used as a pillow, and thereafter he vowed a vow (Genesis 28:20). There is at first no direct speaking to God at all, for God is referred to in the third person. Only at the very end do we get the pronoun "thou" used (verse 22). Jacob would here make conditions with God; Jacob's part is seen as becoming obligatory upon him after God has done His part. Hence this is not to be regarded as a prayer in the proper sense of the term.

A very good example of prayer is found in Jacob's appeal unto God when he was afraid because of the coming of Esau (Genesis 32:9-12). There has been much spiritual progress made by Jacob in the meantime, as we see from his opening words: "O God of my father Abraham, and God of my father Isaac, O LORD." The expressions relating to Abraham and to Isaac recall the covenanted promises to the men whom God has chosen, but it is not simply, "O God of my father Isaac," but there is the direct calling upon the name of the LORD. It is an affirmation of a personal relationship which seems to be lacking in the prayer of Eliezer. This personal relation is still further avouched when he recalls the command of the LORD to return to his own country and kindred. It is a drawing near in all boldness to the One who has manifested his loving-kindness, to the One who had said, "I will do thee good." Now let us note how Jacob, after this opening, makes a confession, of unworthiness and weakness: "I am not worthy of the least of all Thy mercies." This is indeed a lovely example of confession in prayer, and it is fitting that this confession finds an early place.

What did Jacob mean by his expression, "For with my staff I passed over this Jordan; and now I am become two companies"? In one sense it has an obvious meaning, that in his outward journey he was alone and that the mercies of God are shown in the fact of his return with a large company of loved ones and dependents and that he was unworthy of this grace. But this cannot be all, for he mentions two companies. Seeing that his fear and distress (verse 7) caused him to divide his people into two companies so as to give a double chance of escape, we might conclude that Jacob was tentatively confessing that at the end of this receipt of blessing he had made human plans before approaching God for help and guidance. This would be pleading unworthiness not only in a general sense, but in the consciousness of specific weakness. While this may be so, we must note that Jacob had just had the experience of having been met by the angels of God, whom he called "God's host." The name which Jacob gave to the place, "Mahanaim," means two hosts or companies, and it is clear that Jacob realised that the blessings of God were manifest before his eyes, not only in the material things, but also in the spiritual things, a host of dependents upon earth, children that were an heritage of the LORD, round about him like olive plants (Psalms 127, 128), but he had also a host of God's ministers round about, ministering spirits indeed, sent forth to do service for the sake of them that were to inherit salvation (Hebrews 1:14).

It may be that in his flurry he makes the division into two human companies—"I am become two companies"—and that he rather regrets this act, realising afresh when too late that God's assurance had been that there were two companies (one of men and one of angels) to be reckoned on. For let us notice, that Jacob goes on to say that he is not worthy of "all the truth ... shewed unto Thy servant." This word "truth" has not to do with doctrine (i.e., with "truth" as we understand it); the Hebrew word (emeth) is said to be a contracted form of the word 'aman', from which the word amen is derived. The notion conveyed is that of stability, the truth conveyed is that God has revealed his established and unalterable purposes in Abraham, Isaac, and also in Jacob. Some portion of this "truth" Jacob had realised in the sending forth of the host of God, and this point Jacob takes up again, when he rises above all self and pleads on behalf of the mother and the children. This pleading for others takes its right setting after his own confession, and he takes high and lofty ground when he thinks of the children who are the firstborn of the promised seed that was to be as the sand of the sea for multitude. Thus Jacob prays in the light of divine things.

Well might he confess his unworthiness of the Amen that God had purposed concerning him. The exceedingly great and precious promises unto us in the

Amen may well be contrasted in our prayers with our own unworthiness! That same night Jacob's prayer is continued in a very striking fashion, in the incident of the striving with God. The final point has arrived, and Jacob is to be tested in a way that leaves its mark upon him for life. "Jacob was left alone; and there wrestled a man with him until the breaking of the day." It would be incorrect to say that Jacob here takes the initiative; it is God who has come to Jacob rather than Jacob to God; it is God who has laid hold of Jacob. The One who said that His Spirit would not strive with man for ever, for that he also is flesh, is constrained to put forth His divine power to bring to nought the power of the flesh in Jacob. What remained for this broken-down man was to cling to the One who is not only able to bring down, but also to lift up. He has been caused to realise one side of God's power, and the other side, which is made manifest in grace, was not to be revealed without asking. The mighty power of God would not be used to thrust away a clinging soul, whose true strength is now to be made perfect in weakness.

With Jacob it was now and henceforth to be as it was with Paul, to whom the Lord said, "My grace is sufficient for thee: for my power is made perfect in weakness." So also could it have been said by Jacob, as was said by Paul, "Most gladly therefore will I rather glory in my weaknesses, that the power of Christ may rest upon me. Wherefore I take pleasure in weaknesses ... for when I am weak, then am I strong" (2 Corinthians 12:9-10). We see from Genesis 32:32 how the children of Israel reverenced the sign of God's dealings with Jacob, in that they ate not of the sinew of the hip. What prayer shall Jacob offer, now that he is striving with God and is prevailing? Shall he specify this and that? Not so, he asks for blessing, without which he will not let go. There are times when to ask for unspecified blessings is the perfection of wisdom, for God knoweth all, and if He blesses, then we are blessed indeed. It was so with Israel, as we should now call him, for he realised that the blessing which God gave him included preservation from all that would hinder the fulfilment of God's purposes in him, whether from Esau or principalities or powers; from henceforth neither things present nor things to come would be able to separate him from the love of God. Happy are we when we have a like persuasion concerning the love of God in Christ Jesus! (Romans 8:38-39).

FOUR: THE PRAYERS OF MOSES

Seeing that we have excluded from our studies the various occasions in which God takes the initiative in speaking to men, we must perforce pass over many of the communications between God and Moses, for even where the latter replies there is not that voluntary "drawing near" which we have taken as a criterion. Perhaps the first instance of prayer by Moses rendered for us is on the well-known occasion when the Israelites were approaching the Red Sea, with Pharaoh and the Egyptians following hard after them. The children of Israel cried out to Jehovah (Exodus 14:10), no doubt for help, but spoke hard words to Jehovah's minister, that Moses whose wondrous doings by the power of Jehovah had been so well esteemed of them.

It is hard for a man of God to deal with a backbiting people; it was truly only by a strong hand that they were brought forth out of Egypt. God heard their cry, as we see from Joshua 24:7, for in consequence of it He put darkness between the two hosts. But Moses was sorely tried. In public he shows forth his undaunted faith, as he exhorts the people to stand still and see the salvation of the LORD. In private, however, he has to suffer a rebuke by God, in that he had cried out to the LORD without cause (verse 15). "Wherefore criest thou unto Me? Speak unto the children of Israel that they go forward." It was a time for action and not for prayer. While the presence of God was made visible in the pillar and in the cloud it was clear that He was over all, that He had the situation in hand, and that He was the leader to be followed by faith. The removal of the pillar of cloud to a position behind the Israelites was a concession to weakness. The words of Moses are sometimes used to inculcate a kind of super-faith, to stand still and see the salvation of God, but the rebuke to Moses should be taken into consideration. It was certainly an act of faith to stand still under the circumstances, but it was a grander act of faith to go forward. If God is visibly leading, then to stand still "in faith" is almost tantamount to an act of doubt or even disbelief.

To cry unto God for the salvation which God has definitely promised (14:4) is something entirely redundant. It is thus possible to pray, even in apparent faith, when prayer is not called for. The great value of prayer is when it is exercised in its proper place, and a good measure of spiritual discernment is needed in this, lest we pray at wrong times and with wrong motives, lest we pray for help from God when we ought to be getting help from the resources He has already provided for us. In this we can learn from the words of Exodus 18:15, where we see that the people enquired of Jehovah by Moses. This does not mean that because the people or individuals had need of help that Moses necessarily supplicated God for them, for verse 16 tends to show that such enquiries were answered by the statutes and laws. Where God has given instruction in His word He does not expect us to act as though we expected help in a miraculous manner through prayer.

In this connection, I may remark that one often hears the statement: "If I can only get to one meeting during the week, I choose the prayer meeting." It always seems to me that this betrays a misconception of the ways of God, rather than that it shows manifest grace in the individual. Rather does it seem to imply that the individual is in no need of the ministry of the word of God and is always in a ripe condition to approach God on behalf of others and on behalf of the work of the Lord. Such ministry is intended by God to cleanse us, to instruct us, and we may be considered to be well-nourished, spiritually, when we are receiving due nourishment from every joint of the supply (see Ephesians 4: 11-16). The four things which God has joined together in Acts 2:42—the apostles' teaching and fellowship, the breaking of bread, and the prayers—should not be separated. In this matter, the Scripture is true, "A false balance is an abomination to the LORD." We need to keep a balance between receiving ministry and being exercised in prayer. The former helps to bring about that state of experimental righteousness to which I have alluded in connection with the prayers of a righteous man. We can depend upon it that if we have valued what God has already said, then He will value what we desire to say.

After this digression, we return to the record of the prayers of Moses. The pressure of events at Marah (Exodus 15:25), and at Massah and Meribah (Exodus 17:4) led Moses to "cry" unto Jehovah —in the language of Psalm 107 he was at his wits' end and cried unto the LORD in his trouble, but we have no instruction from the form or substance of these cries. The incident of the holding up of the hands of Moses by Aaron and Hur is often used to urge the value of continued prayer, but such teaching as it has is by way of type, for God is not, apparently, directly addressed. But it is so beautiful a picture of intercession that we are constrained to linger over it, for even though we receive no instruction for our prayers, we are caused to realise the great and glorious fact that there is One who ever intercedes for us, and does that when we are least able to pray for ourselves.

The incident is that of Joshua going out to fight against Amalek, a type of the grim warfare that every child of God has to engage in, a type of warfare against the flesh. The daily struggle against the lusts of the body, the flesh, and the mind, is often more than we can bear, knowing that if we live after the flesh we must die. We thank God that He has associated with this struggle His very gracious words, that we have "received the spirit of adoption, whereby we cry, Abba, Father" (Romans 8:15). Further, we rejoice that we read, "In like manner the Spirit also helpeth our infirmity; for we know not how to pray as we ought; but the Spirit Himself maketh intercession for us ... according to the will of God" (Romans 8:26-27). Yet over and above this, when the conflict is raging fiercely, when we have deliberately faced the foe as Joshua did, we can rejoice in the further word, "Who is he that shall condemn? It is Christ Jesus that died, yea rather, that was raised from the dead, who is at the right hand of God, who also maketh intercession for us" (Romans 8:34).

"He ever liveth to make intercession" (Hebrews 7:25) is true, whether of the things we utter or of the things He utters for us. Very beautifully is all this foreshadowed as Moses, with the rod of God in his hand, commits the warfare to Joshua, while he himself, remote from the scene of battle, held up his hands in supplication. The type may fail, but the anti-type never. The hands of Moses might fall, priestly service might need to be rendered by others not engaged in battle, but the supplications of our blessed Lord fail not. Yet how precious is the thought that in priestly service we have also the privilege of aiding this work in offering up our supplications also through Him on behalf of our struggling brethren! Well might Moses erect an altar, and call it, "Jehovah is my banner," the banner never to be furled in the warfare against flesh.

Moses is again brought before us in an intercessory character in Exodus 32. While he had been in the Mount with God, Aaron had let the people loose, and they had begun to worship the golden calf. It was God who first informed Moses of this (verse 7), and asked to be let alone that in His anger He might consume them. The temptation to Moses must have been very great, when God said unto him that in place of Israel he would make of Moses a great nation. "Thy people" (verse 7) was the description of them by God to Moses. It is delightful to read how Moses pleaded with God. It is now his turn to say "Thy people" (verse 11), and he goes on to show his discernment of God's righteous character, and he pleads with Jehovah on this basis, just as Abraham did with regard to Sodom, though the plea is the greater because it was concerning a redeemed and chosen people.

The question of confession of personal sin and frailty does not here arise, seeing that Moses had been so long in the presence of God, but when Moses descended the Mount and saw for himself the sinful condition of the people then it was brought home unto him. "Thy people"—if so he had a double duty, to act and to pray, and the former must come first, for there was no question as to the judgment of God upon the sin of the people. Moses is not again to hear the response, "Why criest thou unto Me?", for there was an immediate work to be done, a purging to be effected. He could then go back to God in fear and trembling, with a peradventure on his lips (verse 30). Though he had pleaded with God concerning a chosen people, he had learnt a great lesson, that to occupy a divine position required a corresponding condition. He does not go now to say to God, "Thy people." It is almost as though he dare not, but he now says, "This people " (verse 31), and he confesses their great sin.

We can only speculate as to the vow that trembled upon his lips as he broke off from saying, "Yet now, if thou wilt forgive their sin—," to visualise unforgiven sin, and to add his desire in that case to be blotted out of "the book." As Adam, though he was not beguiled, partook with Eve of the fruit of her sin, because she was bone of his bone, flesh of his flesh, so Moses was prepared to throw in his lot with the people whom God had called "Thy people." This latter prayer of Moses, we notice, hardly gets beyond confession. Moses seems to be overwrought, both in his suggestions of offering something in return for forgiveness of sin (which is foreign to God's way, for forgiveness comes after the offering, and is not given in return for a vow as yet unfulfilled), and also in his remark about being blotted out of the book. The reply of God is clear and pungent, that He would punish those that sinned, but He accepted for the rest the intercession of Moses. "The people," as God now calls them, were to go on to the place promised unto them, so that God honoured His covenant and His word unto Moses. When sin is very great, and the heart is bowed down under it, the spoken words may only be, "God, be merciful to me a sinner," but the prayer that does not rise above the groundwork of confession is in no ways despised of God, for "if we confess our sins, He is faithful and righteous to forgive us our sins, and to cleanse us from all unrighteousness" (1 John 1:9).

"The Lord spake unto Moses face to face, as a man speaketh unto His friend." Such is the high commendation given unto Moses on more than one occasion. Jacob had experience of this when he strove with God at Peniel (Genesis 32:30), and the Israelites knew something of it when before Mount Sinai (Deuteronomy 5.:4), but none had the same depth of experience as Moses had. Of him, God says, "With him will I speak mouth to mouth, even manifestly, and not in dark speeches" (Numbers 12:8). What is meant by the expression "I know thee by name" (Exodus 33:17) is to me rather obscure unless it is considered in relation to the prayer of Moses in Exodus 33:12-16, which we shall now proceed to discuss.

After the judgment of the people who had broken loose under Aaron, God said that He would not go up in the midst of the people to the promised land, lest He consume them in the way, and an angel was promised who would be sent before the people. Those who sought the LORD went out unto the tent of meeting without the camp, and it was there that the LORD spoke with Moses (33:9). Then we read that Moses said unto the LORD, "See, Thou sayest unto me, Bring up this people: and Thou hast not let me know whom Thou wilt send with me. Yet Thou hast said, I know thee by name, and thou hast found grace in My sight." Moses had a longing desire to know even as he was known and since God Himself was not to be in the midst of the people then Moses longed to know more of the One who was to act on behalf of God.

The Lord Jesus tells us that life eternal is to know the only true God and Him whom God did send, even Jesus Christ (John 17:3), and something of this spirit animated Moses, to be known and to know. Hence he continues, "Now therefore, I pray Thee, if I have found grace in Thy sight, shew me now Thy ways, that I may know Thee, to the end that I may find grace in Thy sight." This is a delightful prayer to ponder. God has already said that Moses had found grace in His sight, yet Moses says, "if." This is not the "if" of doubt, there is no lack of faith here, but the man of God seizes upon the consequence, that if God has so blessed it is only an earnest of further blessing. It is the kind of logic that is very dear to the heart of God, the logic that Paul uses so forcibly in Romans 8:32, "He that spared not His own Son, but delivered Him up for us all, how shall He not also with Him freely give us all things?"

Moses has already had cause to marvel at the grace of God, considering the people who had murmured at the God of Grace; yea, rather, Moses had cause to realise that he himself was weak and liable to err. What shall he ask for, therefore, except to have the ways of God revealed to him, that he might not stumble? "God showed His ways unto Moses, His doings unto the Children of Israel" (Psalm 103:7). What a difference! People who only learn by bitter experience are a trial to themselves and to God, and the Judgment Seat of Christ will reveal the numberless failures owing to the lack of desire to walk in the ways of God. The Psalmist desired to be shown the ways of God, to walk in His paths, and to be guided in the truth and taught by the God of His salvation. Surely the thought of grace received, the occasion of that thankfulness which we have stressed as essential to prayer, should lead us to long after being well pleasing to God. Prayer should lead to something, and the truth of God is set before us as that wherein we can show some return to God for all His grace and lovingkindness.

Apart from the revelation of the Scriptures we can say with Paul that God's ways are past tracing out. But none can say today that the truth of God and the ways of God in some measure are not to be discerned. We are no longer to look for a revelation from God on the matters which are to be found expounded in the word of God. Even so, the longing soul desiring to pray for the ways of God to be made manifest is right in doing so provided he is ready to search what

God has written. God's ways are to be discerned in His Word, and He speaks to us in His Word. It was not so much that Moses spoke to God face to face as that God spoke to Moses. Prayer is not to be a one-sided business. Samuel knew this, as we see from 1 Samuel 12:19-24: "God forbid that I should sin against the LORD in ceasing to pray for you: but I will instruct you in the good and right way." We are not as dependent as they upon the services of another in prayer, when we have the glorious privilege of drawing near to God, but the necessity of instruction in the ways and truth of God is laid upon us.

Happy are we when we take heed to the words of Samuel, and consider how great things God has done for us, so leading us to serve Him in truth. It was for a purpose that Moses asked to know the ways of God, "that I may know Thee." He had spoken with God face to face, and yet he realises that he does not know God. Paul, too, had wonderful experiences with Christ and wonderful revelations of Him, yet we read his desire as expressed to the Philippians, "that I may know Him, and the power of His resurrection ..." This is indeed life eternal that here and now, in these bodies and in these changing scenes, we can know something of God and of the One He has sent. Is this what we long for, or are our prayers taken up with the mundane things, the needs of our bodies and our service? To rise above these and to long to know more of the great God and Creator, the great God of compassion and love, the God and Father of our Lord Jesus Christ, is to get very great value out of prayer.

It is very instructive to note the further purpose in this prayer— it is to the end that Moses might find grace in God's sight. We might think that this is where Moses began. Is he wandering in a circle? No, indeed. The man who knows more of God is intensely desirous of more grace. It is not a circle, Moses at the end is not back where he was at the start; prayer is almost in vain if it consists of repetitions of thoughts and experiences. I liken it to a spiral; after one revolution the outlook is much the same but is on a higher plane. The cycle of experience in prayer begins with grace and ends with grace, but it is that grace which leads us higher, as the hymn beautifully puts it. Paul has the same thought, I judge, in Philippians 3:14 (the whole chapter has connections with the prayer we are studying). He is stretching on, pressing on, to the prize of the upward (RV margin) calling of God in Christ Jesus. Finally, Moses asks the question,

"Wherein now shall it be known that I have found grace in Thy sight, I and the people?"

We would to God that we all might ponder this question. What shall be the criterion? How shall men discern that our God is blessing us abundantly by His grace? We would, too, that all our readers might yearn to give the same answer as Moses gave, an answer apparently beyond the desires of most professing Christians. "Is it not in that Thou goest with us, so that we be separated, I and Thy people, from all the people that are upon the face of the earth?" The pathway of separation cannot be walked by a child of God without much grace from Him. This prayer teaches us to look at separation in an unusual light. We generally regard it as a cross to be borne with such fortitude as we can muster, but Moses teaches us that separation is rather to be gloried in, for it is impossible to maintain it without grace and still more grace. For this reason therefore, we shall do well to ponder again and yet again the four quarters of the cycle—thanksgiving as grace is recalled to mind, the desire to walk in the ways of God, the desire to know more of Him, and the desire for more grace.

We shall deal more fully on a later occasion with the incidents of Numbers 11, and we pass on to note that in Numbers 12., after Aaron and Miriam had spoken against Moses, and God had spoken to them on behalf of Moses, Aaron pleaded with. Moses on behalf of Miriam, and Moses cried unto the LORD, saying, "Heal her, O God, I beseech Thee." This request was denied by God so far as immediate cure was concerned. Even Moses could not ask contrary to the law of God, teaching us the lesson we have already had, that we must seek to ask according to the mind and will of God. From the incidents of Numbers 21, where the Israelites were bitten by fiery serpents, we see the importance attached to confession of sin before prayer can be made and granted. The people said "We have sinned ...; pray unto the LORD." The answer is immediately given.

The last prayer of Moses recorded in the Scriptures is in Numbers 27. Moses is to be allowed to go up into the mountain to see the Land, and his sin at the waters of Meribah is recalled to him by God. His only request is that the LORD, "the God of the spirits of all flesh," will appoint a man over the congregation, that it be not as sheep which have no shepherd. The shepherd care that Moses had for the people of God rules in his heart to the very end. We may note the wisdom of Moses. It must have been obvious that only Joshua was fitted to be the leader, but it is not even a Moses who appoints. There is something particularly lovely here as the meekest of all men does not presume to suggest a name to God. "The LORD seeth not as man seeth; for man looketh on the outward appearance, but God looketh on the heart." We can learn something from this, not to be too particularising in our requests. The same lesson was learnt from the experience of Jacob when he asked for blessing, and left it at that.

FIVE: MOSES, A DISCOURAGED MAN OF GOD

There is nothing like having to endure discouragement that tests the believer almost to the limit of endurance, like the Psalmist of Psalm 73 who confessed that his feet had almost gone, his steps had well nigh slipped, as he considered the apparent prosperity of the wicked and the troubles besetting the pure and innocent. It is when one has felt that one has laboured hard to be well-pleasing unto God and yet trials and difficulties are our lot that murmurings arise in the heart and complaints find expression by the tongue. The joy seems then to depart from our prayers and it is in these trying circumstances that we are prone to make mistakes in our prayers.

This was the experience of many of God's great servants in the Old Testament, and it is indeed remarkable to notice how even these mighty men of old allowed expressions to pass their lips that were clearly displeasing to God. Moses had an experience of this kind in Numbers 11. In the preceding chapter we have the record of his dealings with Hobab, in which we have a lovely expression of his assurance that God intended to do good unto His people. It was not Moses in the first place who was discouraged by the difficulties of the wilderness journey, but the people lusted and murmured. At the outset they had no specific grievance. Murmuring is a very great evil. It is like an infectious disease, especially when there is no definite cause of dissatisfaction which can be dealt with. Alas, when brethren grumble and grumble and murmur! Before long they infect others, and the pity is that murmuring is like certain children's diseases, which are most dangerous to others before the spots appear and the true character of the disease is made apparent.

There are some who have this disease in a mild and chronic fashion, but those who are affected by them may oft-times catch the complaint with fatal results. The writer knows of at least one brother lost to the people of God because he caught the habit of murmuring from another brother. Moreover, it is not only thus that evil is caused. It is very true that we do not live to ourselves nor die to ourselves, and the result was that Moses was thrown off his balance, as on a previous occasion, and was led to speak unadvisedly with his lips, and that to God. Please read the prayer uttered by Moses in his displeasure (Numbers 11:11-15).

His discouragement is great indeed when he desires rather to be killed out of hand than to be called upon to endure the care of the people under the circumstances. Note the entire absence of thanksgiving! Where is the confession? Where is the discernment of the character of God? All the things we have considered together as being vital to acceptable prayer are lacking. Note too the recurring " I ... I ... I ..." This is characteristic of the prayers of discouraged men, as indeed is to be expected seeing that a man who is absolutely convinced of the power and grace of God can never be discouraged. The flesh is indeed weak, and in this exhibition of its weakness we should expect the flesh to be unduly evident. The Psalmist, when he has realised the truth of his condition, says, "So brutish was I, and ignorant; I was as a beast before Thee" (Psalm 73:22).

The answer of the LORD to this prayer is very significant in it indirectness. Though He had originally been greatly angry with the people, He first deals with Moses, and that in a striking fashion. It had been the good pleasure of God to commune with Moses face to face, and He had never been lacking when there was need for counsel. It was simply untrue that Moses was bearing the responsibility of the people by himself, and the LORD shows to Moses that His grace had been sufficient indeed. Moses is caused to bring 70 elders unto the tent of meeting that they might share the burden with Moses. We may note that on an earlier occasion Moses accepted the advice of Jethro and appointed 70 men to assist in the administration of the affairs of the people, but then there was no question of loss of position to Moses.

Now God takes of the spirit already upon Moses and places it upon the elders, a lesson to Moses that the grace of God had truly been sufficient indeed, and that God had amply provided for his every need. The result is that these elders are found prophesying in the tent of meeting. What a lesson to Moses to see the transforming power of the Spirit! Hitherto He had been the one to express the mind of God and to exhort the people as to the goodness and the grace of God, but now he is caused to see that no man is indispensable and that God taketh up whom He will, that no power exists but what is of God. We note that they did so no more, and we take this to mean that the lesson was for Moses, a lesson that the true remedy for discouragement is in prophesying. Further, we have the remarkable work of Eldad and Medad as they prophesied in the camp. The fact that Joshua was so impressed by this that he asked Moses to forbid them is a testimony to the power of the utterances of these men, utterances that had hitherto come only from the lips of Moses, for he alone could be said to have known the character and purposes of God; God showed His ways unto Moses.

The reply of Moses, "Would God that all the LORD'S people were prophets, that the LORD would put His Spirit upon them!" shows that Moses had had a very remarkable lesson. In fact, we can say that he was no longer a discouraged man. It is good for us to dwell a little upon the incidents in the camp. We are not told what Eldad and Medad said to the people, but we may meditate upon the meanings of their names. It is generally said that Eldad means "God is a friend," and Medad means "Love." This is suggestive, but not altogether satisfactory, since there are other words translated thus. The letters "dad" common to both names, taking into account also that "El" is known to refer to God, suggests a line of thought. Lexicons differ very much in their suggestions as to the derivations of these two names, but if we note that the word "dad " means "a breast," our thoughts are immediately taken to verse 12, where Moses asks why God should desire him to carry this people in his bosom, as a nursing-father carrieth the sucking child.

The suggestion is that what Moses was not desirous of being, God was prepared to be! It stirs one's mind to think of these two men asking the people of Israel to consider the LORD as a friend indeed, such a friend that He thinks of them as a child upon His bosom; having such love that He tenderly cares for them and provides for their needs. It was bringing God as a Father before them, and we may say that a murmuring man and a discouraged man have got out of touch with God as a Father. These men all prophesied. Murmurers cannot be helped otherwise, for they need the three things which characterise prophesying: edification, comfort, and consolation. It is in such terms that prophesying is defined in 1 Corinthians 14:3.

The discouraged Psalmist of Psalm 73, after he had realised his wrong condition, says, "Nevertheless I am continually with Thee; Thou hast holden my right hand." This is comfort of a high order. This refers to the fatherly care of God.

"Thou shalt guide me with Thy counsel." This is edification indeed. If God is with us, does it matter who is against us? If we have been discouraged hitherto, will not the perfect counsel of God bring us full satisfaction? "And afterward receive me to glory." This is true consolation. The wicked may prosper and be free from many of the trials and difficulties which we have to endure, but in the end it will all be made up to us in the glory. There is a work that can be done "in the camp," when saints speak to one another the comfort which is in Christ. We each have a responsibility in this matter to be of help to our fellows. Let us beware of getting discouraged, lest we find ourselves on a slippery slope from which we shall only be recovered after God has dealt with us as he dealt with Moses. Above all, let us be thankful, and remember the many mercies of God.

SIX: THE DESPONDENCY OF JOSHUA

Joshua's experiences in connection with Ai (Joshua 7) are full of instruction for believers, associated as those experiences are with weakness and defeat, the circumstances in which prayer is most called for and most appreciated by the suppliant conscious both of his own need and the resources of his God. At the end of chapter 6 we read, "So the LORD was with Joshua, and his fame was in all the land."

This may well mean that the fame of Jehovah was in all the land, but Joshua would have been more than human if he had not felt that he also had acquired a certain amount of fame. Humility is not the easiest lesson to learn when the servant of God is clearly being much blessed of God, and experience teaches that most of us are vulnerable to the attacks of the adversary when we are most jubilant about the great victories won. Then we are prone to go on in our own strength and wisdom to learn in the bitter school of adversity that we need a continual supply of divine energy to do a divine work. Clearly, Joshua had not sought the counsel of God in the further work of subduing the land of Canaan, or he would have discerned that the anger of the LORD was kindled against the children of Israel. He seeks the advice of mere men, the spies who go up to the mountain and make the opposite error of the spies who were first sent out by Moses.

The latter spies over-rated the power of the inhabitants of the land and under-rated the power of God, but these later spies make the fatal mistake of underestimating the number and might of the men of Ai. Their estimate was about three thousand men, though in the sequel as many as twelve thousand men and women of Ai were slain. It is fatal for a believer to under-estimate the power of the adversary- One would have thought that Joshua had had enough experience of the work of spies to have lasted him a life-time. So Joshua and the elders of Israel rent their clothes and fell on their faces before the Ark of the LORD until the evening, and put dust upon their heads. This is sometimes used as an example of continuance in prayer, but the true test of its value is in what is thought and said. Joshua takes time for thought, and that before God.

Were his thoughts like those of the Psalmist in Psalm 48? "We have thought on thy lovingkindness, O God, in the midst of Thy temple. As is Thy name, O God, so is Thy praise unto the ends of the earth: Thy right hand is full of righteousness." The modern pilgrim, picturing himself in a desert drear and wild, can sing: "Thoughts of His love, the root of every grace, That finds in this poor heart a dwelling place."

But poor Joshua, alas, is very discouraged and forgets to think of the many mercies he and the people had received, and thankfulness finds no place in his thoughts so that thanksgiving finds no place in his prayer. The salt is lacking and the prayer is without savour before God. Read what he is led to say after so much thought. "Alas, O LORD God, wherefore hast Thou at all brought this people over Jordan ... to cause us to perish." There is no discernment here of the righteous and merciful character of God. Such an imputation is without justification, and is followed by an expression which is similar in thought to that which has afflicted many believers in all ages: "Would that we had been content and dwelt beyond Jordan!" If we are to learn from the experiences of Joshua, we must frankly admit that a disciple of the Lord Jesus, when experiencing the difficulties of the way, is easily caused by the adversary to wish that he had never taken the step of separation, that he had never chosen the narrow way when the broad and easy way of sectarianism offers so much ease of mind. To have stayed beyond Jordan was precisely what Satan would have desired for the people of God. "Would that we have been content!"

Is there a believer who has not had to face this suggestion again and yet again? We are more blessed than Joshua in that we have the Holy Spirit dwelling within us to whisper in our hearts the tale of grace, to keep our thoughts centred upon the Lord of Glory who also wandered in this vale of tears, and experienced sinless suffering and patient grace, whose grace is mingled with His glory—that "Beacon of hope, which, lifted up on high, Illumes with heavenly light the tear-dimmed eye." Joshua goes on to express fear of the people being cut off from the earth, and asks the question, "And what wilt Thou do for Thy great name?" While it is good to have thought for the honour and glory of God, we pander to human weakness and pride whenever we think that God is absolutely dependent upon us, the recipients of His grace. By the mercy of God we are His people and He delights to have us to serve Him, but we do well to remember that no man, no people, is indispensable to God. He was prepared to make a nation of Moses, to begin again in him. When He was rejected by the Jews He was prepared to begin again with the Gentiles, and the Lord said to the Children of Abraham, "God is able of these stones to raise up children to Abraham." God will see to it that He will get Him honour for His name.

Is it any wonder, therefore, that the reply of God to all this is, "Get thee up; wherefore art thou thus fallen upon thy face? Israel hath sinned ..." There is indeed such a thing as "prayer in its proper place"; apart from the character of what is said there are certain things which need attention, as we pointed out in connection with one of the prayers of Moses. Self-examination is a very valuable exercise preliminary to prayer, and indeed in the act of worship and the gifts laid upon the altar. The principles of Matthew 5 and 18 relative to the settlement of difficulties between brethren before gifts can be laid upon the altar in a righteous manner are extremely important. If we were more concerned with self-judgment we should find ourselves more acceptable in prayer. When we know that there are matters of righteousness which need urgent attention, can we go to God with a good conscience and hide the facts in His presence? Self-examination - we stressed the importance of this in our earlier chapters.

With all his many thoughts, Joshua had not asked himself whether the fault was in himself or in the people, but had assumed that God was at fault. So far as he was concerned, there might have been nothing to reproach himself with, but he had the responsibility of a people. He was the bishop or overseer of that day, in that he had to watch over the souls of the people. It was in this respect that he had erred in not ascertaining whether the people had sinned in the devoted thing. Even though Achan had sinned and kept the matter private, it would have been possible for Joshua to have asked himself and God if the calamity at Ai was indeed due to the sins of the people. So careful is the LORD to emphasise the human responsibility in this matter that He does not reveal unto Joshua the name of the culprit, but recourse has to be made to casting lots, leading to the sin being fixed upon Achan. It is now Joshua's responsibility to deal with Achan, and it is interesting to read what he says to Achan (verse 19): "My son, give, I pray thee, glory to the LORD, the God of Israel, and make confession unto Him."

These things had been lacking in the despondent Joshua, but now he is in a happier and wiser condition. Give glory ... make confession unto God ... and hide not the matter from men! We may digress for a moment to consider the culprit. The temptation was great, but now his sin has found him out, and he knows that he must pay the penalty. Alone in his sin, he is not alone in the penalty, for he and all that he had, sons and daughters among them, were consumed before the wrath of God. What, one wonders, were Achan's thoughts concerning the thirty-six men who had lost their lives when fleeing from the men of Ai? One man sins and another suffers: this is made abundantly evident in the Scriptures. David sinned in numbering the people and seventy thousand men of Israel suffered the loss of their lives in the pestilence. No man lives to himself and no man dies to himself. One member suffers and all the members are affected. Would that all the children of God would realise this in greater measure!

The further dealings of God with Joshua in this matter are full of grace. There is not to be any mistake in undervaluing the enemy. "Take all the men of war" is the command to Joshua in that day, even as the exhortation in this day is to "put on the whole armour of God" that we may fight against the world-rulers of this darkness and the spiritual hosts of wickedness in the heavenly places (Ephesians 6:12). Then the word of counsel is given; "set thee an ambush for city behind it." This is better far than the counsel of men. The best guide we can have in fighting the good fight is the Word of God." Every purpose is established by counsel; and by wise guidance make thou war" (Proverbs 20:18). Note, too, the grace of God in allowing the people this time to take the spoil of the city for themselves. At the close of the day, Joshua is careful to obey the commands of the LORD, in that at the going down of the sun he commanded that the body of the king of Ai be taken down from the tree whereon he had been hanged (Deuteronomy 21:23). "Then Joshua built an altar unto the LORD." Here we leave the man who has been taught of God, a happier and a wiser man, having learnt a lesson in the school of God.

SEVEN: HANNAH AND SAMUEL

Hannah is a conspicuous example of a suppliant conscious of very deep distress of mind and seeking help from God. We can only conjecture the reason why the LORD had shut up her womb (1 Samuel 1:5), though we have the general instruction that whom the LORD loves He chastens. God certainly had not approved of the favour shown by Jacob to Rachel relatively to Leah, as we see from the grace shown by God towards Leah in the matter of children. "Leah was hated" and the fault lay with Jacob, and many years rolled on before Rachel was remembered. We read that God hearkened unto her (Genesis 30:17) even as he had aforetime hearkened to Leah (verse 17). Yet Leah's descendant, Elkanah, seems not to have remembered these things.

God hearkened! We might well wonder how many years were spent by Hannah in this grief, but clearly the distress was especially manifested "year by year" (verse 7) and the association with the visit to the House of the LORD is stressed for our attention. Why Peninnah was so bitter on these occasions might be put down to the favour shown by Elkanah as he distributed portions of the sacrifice. "Year by year" reminds us of the experience of David in 2 Samuel 21:1 when the famine was sore over the land for three years, "year after year," and at the end we read that David sought the LORD. God hearkens, but sometimes He waits until we realise that there is need to approach Him, and it may be that year by year Hannah went up to the House of the LORD and did not think to beseech the God of the House. She was learning in the school of God, and some of the lessons are only learnt in tears and sorrow of heart. When we are at our wits' end, then we cry to the LORD in our trouble, and the LORD hears our cry and delivers us out of our troubles.

We may note that Hannah was in bitterness of soul; then she prayed unto the LORD: then she wept sore, and finally she made a vow. We are given the terms of the vow, but we are not given the details of the prayer. We pointed out in the first chapter that a vow is not a prayer and that the Scriptures distinguish between prayers and vows. A vow should be preceded by the sacrifice of thanksgiving, and we draw attention to this because we feel that the importance of thanksgiving should not be lost sight of. What is said in the vow in nowise can be said to correspond to the expression used by Hannah to Eli: "I poured out my soul to the LORD." Hannah's experiences are well expressed by the first part of Psalm 42, where also we read of one pouring out his soul. Like him, her tears had been her meat day and night as Peninnah, perhaps, had taunted her and continually said unto her, "Where is thy God?" These things Hannah remembered, in the words of the Psalm, as she went with the throng to the House of God, with the voice of joy and praise, a multitude keeping holyday.

Well might she also have asked "Why are thou cast down, O my soul? And why art thou disquieted within me? Hope thou in God: for I shall yet praise Him For the help of His countenance" (RV margin) Yet her's was the experience of knowing that "The LORD will command His lovingkindness in the day-time, and in the night His song shall be with me, even a prayer unto the God of my life." So she also poured out her soul to God, and she went her way, and her countenance was no more sad. Now let it be noted that "her countenance was no more sad " is an expression dating from this pouring out of her soul, the offering of her vow, and the blessing of the priest Eli. This happy condition was realised long before she received that for which she had prayed, a matter which is too often lost sight of in our thoughts on this episode. The fact is, that the value of prayer often lies in the contact with God rather than in the realisation of the desired blessing. The healing influences of the divine presence are beyond all calculation. Nevertheless God blessed her and gave her the desire of her heart.

The prayer of Hannah recorded in Chapter 2 is of a different character from that we have been speaking of. It is a prayer of exultation rather than of distress. Her first prayer thus illustrates the characteristics of prayer in association with weakness and need, and the discerning of the character of God as a present help in time of trouble. Her second prayer is illustrative of the desirability of discerning the character of God as we come with thanksgiving. Hannah exulted! There could be no question as to the reality of her thankful spirit, and, as we have said again and again, this is a very necessary spirit. Like most prayers which begin with thanksgiving there is a transition to praise. The "judging", which is implied in the word "prayer" when applied to the LORD, leads to praise. As Hannah exults in the LORD she exalts her voice in Him. Exultation and exaltation are wondrous words to associate together, and these are the words which characterise this prayer.

"He raiseth up the poor out of the dust, He lifteth up the needy from the dunghill, to make them sit with princes, and inherit the throne of glory." Here is exaltation, and it should provoke exultation in us who have known what it is to be lifted up and seated with Christ in heavenly places. But if exaltation produces that thankful heart which brings forth exultation, so we have the converse, when exultation in the presence of God lifts us out of the plane of earth and on to the plane of heaven, as we realise what it means to possess the peace of God. So we read:

> "Blessed is the people that know the joyful sound: They walk, O LORD, in the light of thy countenance. In Thy name do they rejoice all the day: And in Thy righteousness are they exalted. For Thou art the glory of their strength: And in Thy favour our horn shall be exalted."

Psalm 89, from which the above quotation is taken, goes on to speak of David as the anointed one, and of the Son of David. It is very remarkable to notice, at the close of Hannah's prayer, how she speaks of "His king" when as yet there was no thought of a king in Israel, let alone of the One who has received the highest exaltation, who, more than all others, has known the secrets lying in the associated words of exultation and exaltation.

Samuel

In Samuel we see a man of prayer indeed. Probably there was none among the prophets of God like him in this. Along with Moses and Aaron, he is specially mentioned as among them that called upon the Name of God (Psalm 99:6-8). He knew the necessity of self-judgment before God was to be approached in prayer, as we see from 1 Samuel 7:1-5 and the confession as regards sin by the Israelites is an indication of the instruction given by Samuel. Again, in verse 8, we have an acknowledgment of Samuel's character as a man of prayer. When Israel asked for a king Samuel prayed to the LORD (8:6), it is very lovely to read the reply of Samuel to the people in 12:23, after he had reproved the people for their sin in asking for a king: " Moreover, as for me, God forbid that I should sin against the LORD in ceasing to pray for you." Such a spirit as this is becoming to all the Lord's people as we pray for one another, but it is also lovely to note the additional remark of Samuel: "But I will instruct you in the good and right way."

It is well for us all to note the wisdom of this, as we have before remarked, that prayer should have the appropriate accompaniments of self-judgment and desire to hear the word of God to us. Looking at a Concordance we see that the words "pray" and "prayed" are very infrequent prior to the first Book of Samuel, and if we consider the intimate connections existing between Hannah, Samuel, and David, we may give an honourable place to Hannah who first learnt the value of prayer, and no doubt taught Samuel to do so, while he, in his turn, left an example to David which most likely was duly noted by that man after God's own heart, and so the divine instruction proceeds from one to another, either by example or precept. "The prayer of the upright is His delight."

EIGHT: THE PRAYERS OF DAVID

The experiences of David are very rich in instruction, both as to the value of prayer in time of need and as to the consequences of the neglect of prayer, for we must admit that even a cursory study of the life of David shows him as a man of contrasting moods and experiences. He often fell very low but the secret of his acceptance with God was partly in this, that he was able to discern his errors and he had a heart desirous of being cleared from hidden faults, while if the task of discernment had been beyond him he had that lovely spirit which responded to the truth when his conduct was reproved by others. If he knew what it was to be brought low, he also knew Him who was the lifter up of his head (Psalm 3).

There are long periods in the life of David when there is no indication that he was lifting up his voice in the morning, and ordering his prayer unto his King and his God (Psalm 5). When, for instance, he was living in the land of the Philistines, and daily telling untruths to the King of Gath, he was hardly in the spirit for approaching to Him of whom he says in Psalm 139, "Thou understandest my thought afar off. Thou searchest out my path and my lying down, And art acquainted with all my ways." It is impossible to draw near to God and speak of our needs, and make request to Him for blessing, and at the same time to think that we can hide from Him the defects of our lives and ways. It is incumbent upon us to remember who God is, and there can never be true self-judgment and confession appropriate to prayer without there also being repentance of our shortcomings. Hence we conclude that while David on the second occasion was in the land of the Philistines he was not a praying man.

During his first flight to Achish, King of Gath, he actually told untruths to the Priest and did not respond to the suggestions of approach to God which were always associated with the ephod. He was not seeking help from God, this man who was fleeing away from the place where he had witnessed the power of God in making even his greatest enemy, Saul, to prophesy, and it was not until he was brought very low and was constrained to feign madness that he seems to have realised his deplorable condition. But let it be noted that he then "sought the

LORD" as we see from Psalm 34, that wonderful commentary on the goodness of God which is shown to those who trust in Him. David was a man who had discerned his errors, and in the next few months we often read of him enquiring of God by the ephod. It is difficult for mere men to keep on the lofty plane of Psalm 34, however, and in course of time we find David saying in his heart that he would one day perish by the hand of Saul, and that there was nothing better for him than to escape into the land of the Philistines.

It was only by the grace of God that he was brought out of the peculiar position in which he found himself, about to fight against the LORD's people. Moreover, before he was to be again in a right condition he had to pass through the bitterness of Ziklag, his people and his goods all having been raided by the Amalekites. When his men turned against him, he remembered that one who had been aforetime a tower of refuge to him, and "David strengthened himself in the LORD his God." Then he called for the ephod and enquired of the LORD. Again, we read of a period of three years in David's later years when God had withheld blessing from Israel, and there was a famine in the land. What, one wonders, were the exercises of David in such a matter? It was not until three years had elapsed that he enquired of Jehovah concerning this affliction. We mention these lapses that we might realise that God has allowed these things to be placed on record that we might take warning.

The man who knew the value of prayer to an outstanding degree was made to realise in correspondingly great measure what he lost when he failed to cry unto his God. In contrast to these things we have in the Psalms a lovely record of the out-pourings of David's heart before his God. Again and again we have the expression that he cried and God answered, but in Psalm 3 we see that those around him went so far as to say that there could not be any help for him in God. Under these circumstances we read how that he cried unto God, who answered him out of His holy hill (a remarkable expression for the occasion), and then with sublime confidence in the One who was a shield for him against the ten thousands who had set themselves against him, we read, "I laid me down and slept." Again, in the next Psalm, we have similar experiences: "Many there be that say, Who will shew us any good?", causing David to desire the light of God's countenance.

Then we get the contrast which has a lesson for the believers of all time: "Thou hast put gladness in my heart, More than they have when their corn and wine are increased." Surely such a confession of joy and thankfulness was pleasing unto God! Again in perfect faith, David says, "In peace will I both lay me down and sleep." This glad result of prayer follows, however, upon certain important preliminaries. In verse 3, David says, "But know that the LORD hath set apart him that is godly for Himself," and it is with this knowledge of the character of God that he adds, in perfect faith, "The LORD will hear when I call upon Him." God hears the prayer of faith, and He hears the supplications of the righteous, "He will fulfil the desire of them that fear Him." If the life is not a life of godliness the urgent necessity of confession of sins must under no circumstances be glossed over.

This point is brought out by David in the next verse: "Stand in awe, and sin not: Commune with your own heart upon your bed, and be still." Where there is self-judgment, confession, thanksgiving, and rejoicing, there is something offered up to God which is very pleasing to Him, and to such a prayer will He hearken. That which is acceptable unto God —surely we ought to consider the two-fold character of prayer. Communion with God is for mutual joy, and when He discerns in us that we have discerned the value of His grace and the beauty of His holiness and the riches of His glory, then that which we offer to Him in prayer is something more than a petition for personal blessings. When prayer merges into praise, then we get that which David beautifully expresses as the desire of his soul: "Let my prayer be set forth as incense before Thee: The lifting up of my hands as the evening sacrifice" (Psalm 141:2).

The value which God attaches to prayers rightly conceived and presented before Him is also seen in Revelation 5:8 and 8:3-4. Prayer is called "the sacrifice of thanksgiving" (Psalm 116:17), with which are associated the "vows." We pointed out in our first chapter that in Psalm 50 there is a demand for the payment of vows prior to the answering of prayer, and we see from Psalm 61 that David clearly realised that a man having been into the presence of God as a suppliant should feel a desire for offering some return to God for the benefits received, and that when one has dedicated time or money or aught else to the service of God he should be faithful in this "vow." Note his desire before the

God who has heard his vows that he might daily perform them. When there has been expressed the desire for mercy and grace it is indeed only fitting that there should be inwrought "every desire of goodness" finding expression in "works of faith." Though it is clear that David could enter very deeply into the meaning of prayer, and though we have sought to deepen our appreciation of the principles governing acceptable prayer, it is noteworthy that when David "sat before the LORD" (2 Samuel 7:18), and gave thanks for the grace of God in connection with great promises as to David's House, the language used is very simple and direct, thus showing that prayer does not need to be elaborate in thought or language provided it is based upon sound principles.

NINE: THE PRAYERS OF SOLOMON

It has been given to few to have had such an experience as Solomon had when the LORD appeared unto him in a dream by night and said, "Ask what I shall give thee" (1 Kings 3:4). Solomon, however, had already learnt the blessing of giving to the LORD, a thousand burnt offerings testifying his appreciation of what was due to his God. Many ask, and receive, and are content to be recipients of the grace of God without sacrifice on their part. Not so with Solomon. He gave liberally to his God and when he had received grace from God in the dream, on awakening he gave again burnt offerings to God (verse 15) and also peace offerings in which God and the priests and Solomon and his household and his friends would have a share. In addition he made a feast to his servants.

So the man who is blessed of God through prayer shares the gifts with others, illustrating the principle that prayer should have deeper motives and wider results than blessing merely for oneself. Solomon has left us a lesson in asking, in that personal blessings are sought principally in connection with the purposes of God in him. He has been made ruler over a people, "Thy people," the people of God. It would be salutary indeed for us to remember in our prayers that we are in this world and in the Fellowship of God's Son for purposes known to God and in some measure known to ourselves. Shall we pray for health? Yes, that we might use it in the service which has been appointed to us. Shall we pray for wealth or even moderate material gain? Again, yes, if in our prayer we dedicate it to the service of our God and leave it to Him to decide whether it be good for us and His service to have it.

No such blessings as these have been promised to us and we have no certainty that God would give them, for He alone knows what is good for us. Thus Solomon asked for none of these things, but he asked for an understanding heart, and it pleased God well. According to James 1:5, wisdom can be asked for with expectation of receiving it, provided we ask for it in faith. We may note in this prayer also that at the outset Solomon recalled the blessings granted unto his father, David, and we know that it is becoming unto a suppliant to remember benefits received. Again, Solomon acknowledged his weakness before God, a matter which is at least helpful to the suppliant to remember.

One of the lengthiest prayers recorded in the Old Testament is that which was offered by Solomon at the dedication of the Temple (2 Chronicles 6). We should get a totally wrong conception of the purpose of this House if we confined our attention to the import of the prayer. The emphasis here is upon the House as a House of prayer; God has a dwelling and there He is to be found by His people, and not only so, but even praying towards the House from afar off is encouraged. It is thus very important to note the great importance attached to prayer in association with the House of God, but to give this the only place in our thoughts would be disastrous. There are some who delight to remember the scripture, "Mine House shall be called an house of prayer for all nations " (Isaiah 56:7), who wilfully ignore the prior scriptures in the same verse: "Even them will I bring to My holy mountain, And make them joyful in My house of prayer; Their burnt offerings and their sacrifices shall be accepted upon mine altar: For mine house shall be called an House of prayer ..."

This is said of the strangers that join themselves to the LORD, to minister unto Him, ... to be His servants. It is such that receive the promise that they should not be separated from the people of God (verse 3), who are firstly to be brought to the Place of the Name, and then to be made joyful. There is never any suggestion in the Scriptures for gifts and blessing only to flow one way, from God to the believer and not conversely. The very fact of having received blessing through prayer should indeed call for a response from the recipient of that blessing, to respond in the way appointed by God, in the giving of spiritual sacrifices in the House of God. Now Solomon knew this well, as we see from 2 Chronicles 2: "Now Solomon purposed to build an house for the name of the LORD, and an house for his kingdom." From the words to Hiram, King of Tyre, we see that the emphasis is upon the offerings to be made (verse 4) and in verse 6 Solomon says, "Who am I then, that I should build Him an house, save only to burn incense before Him? " This was the true motive, and the result was a house which was not only for the name of the LORD, but was also a house for the kingdom; an house which man made for God became a place of mutual blessing.

At the dedication of the House the people were made to realise that this house wherein God deigned to dwell was designed to make the presence of God in their midst a very real thing so far as their apprehension of it went, and that when He deigned to dwell among them He desired to hear their prayers and supplications that He might bless them. The more conscious they were of this fact the more they would turn to Him in prayer, and so it is with us. We have the Holy Spirit dwelling in us and the more we are conscious of this the more we desire to draw near to God. Again, the consciousness of being in the House of God that exists upon the earth today should lead to more frequent and fervent prayer. This follows upon the fundamental principle of prayer, that prayer consists of judgment, as we pointed out in our first chapter, and we see this from the opening words of Solomon, as he begins with an appreciation of the Person and character of God (2 Chronicles 6:14). Then he goes on to remember the promises made to David and recalls that those promises have been and are being fulfilled.

On this basis he proceeds to entreat the favour of God towards his servants who should pray in or towards this place. He mentions typical circumstances which can be summarised as follows:

1. The sinner swearing falsely before the altar (verses 22-23), The house is a place of judgment and if a man will not judge the character of God aright as he comes before Him, then he must expect judgment and not mercy. It is useless for us to pray unto God and seek to hide our wrongdoing.

2. The people sinning and only realising this as they are defeated by their enemies.

3. The sin of the people realised as the blessings of heaven are withdrawn, and famine desolates the land.

4. Similar realisation of sin as various calamities befall the people.

5. The stranger coming from a far country for the sake of the Name.

6. Going out in service to war, seeking help.

7. The people delivered into captivity because of sin.

Of these seven cases, all but two are concerned with the consequences of sin, and a prominent place is given to the necessity for repentance, confession, and prayer. In verse 29 it speaks of every man knowing his own plague and his own sorrow, as he spreads forth his hands towards the house of God. Prayer truly arises out of the realisation of need and impotence, and self-examination is desirable rather than waiting until sin has borne such fruit that the need becomes dire indeed. Again Solomon takes up the point that though God may forgive, yet He renders unto every man according to his ways, and not altogether according to his asking (verse 30), and we are warned that in these things God judges according to the heart of a man, a judgment infallible indeed, for nothing can be hidden from Him. Thus we have in this prayer of Solomon the lesson we have had on previous occasions, that our drawing near to God in prayer should have the result that we have fresh resolves of heart, especially to seek to do the will of God as it is revealed to us. If this is thoroughly understood we should be less often praying vain repetitions.

Especially would we stress on this occasion that every believer today who approaches his God in prayer should understand that there is a good and perfect will of God revealed in the Scriptures, that today He has a house upon earth, a house not made of inanimate stones, but built of living stones, that there are services in this house, and that it is the will of God that prayer should be associated with the house in that all prayer is heard and accepted through Him who is Priest over God's house. In our ignorance we may not have realised that today, as in Solomon's day, it is the God of the house who answers prayer. Happy are we if we have been diligent to enter into this truth.

TEN: THE PRAYERS OF DANIEL, EZRA, AND NEHEMIAH

It is evident that Daniel, Ezra, and Nehemiah, were men whose thoughts turned, we are going to say, almost instinctively to prayer in moments of crisis. But to use such an expression undervalues the character of these men, for it can almost be said of men in general that they instinctively turn to God when in need or distress: "Then they cry unto the LORD in their trouble" (Psalm 107). It would lead us to go beyond our scope and knowledge, however, to define instinct. "The spirit of man is the lamp of the Lord searching all the innermost parts of the belly" (Proverbs 20. 27). The word of God is a lamp unto our feet (Psalm 119:105), and Job delighted in the way in which God shone upon him:

> "Oh that I were as in the months of old, as in the days when God watched over me; when His lamp shined upon my head, and by His light I walked through darkness; as I was in the ripeness of my days, when the secret of God was upon my tent" (Job 29:2-4).

These lamps are external, but the lamp of which we write is internal. In the Tabernacle of old the lamp testified that God watched over His people, and that He was alive to their existence. So this lamp which is the spirit of man testifies within us as to the existence of God, but it is His lampstand and we might well ponder the thought of that light exploring all the recesses of our minds and souls. This being the function of the spirit of man, we turn to Psalm 44:20-21 to read of the searching of God: If we have forgotten the name of our God, Or spread forth our hands to a strange god; Shall not God search this out? For He knows the secrets of the heart.

There can be no comparison between the immature and ignorant feelings which we associate with instinct and those which come from instruction in the things of God, such instruction as is evident had been accorded to Daniel, Ezra, and Nehemiah. These men turned at once to the God whom they knew, whether it was in connection with the urgent necessities arising from the dream of Nebuchadnezzar, which led Daniel at once to seek the help of his friends in prayer (Daniel 2:18), or whether in connection with the journeys of Ezra and Nehemiah, or as to how Nehemiah should answer the king. The lamp of the LORD never shines in all its fullness without some effort on our parts. If it is possible to quench the Spirit, how much easier it is to hinder the working of the spirit of man! Though God may know the secrets of the heart, none among men may know them save the spirit of the man himself (1 Corinthians 1:11), and it is the operation of the Holy Spirit upon our spirit which takes us out of the category of the natural man who can never receive the things of the Spirit of God (1 Corinthians 1:14). They must be foolishness to him, because they are spiritually judged.

This same Holy Spirit is a searcher also, in the deep things of God, and the man that is instructed by Him becomes a searcher also: "I have considered the days of old, the years of ancient times ... I commune with mine own heart; And my spirit made diligent search" (Psalm 77:5-6). We might almost imagine Daniel reading this beautiful Psalm of Asaph, and saying with him, "Will the LORD cast off for ever? ... Hath God forgotten to be gracious?" Howbeit, Daniel was led to consider the woes of his people in captivity and was ultimately led to search the Scriptures for that light and guidance which comes from them alone, and in due course found that which had been plainly written, but had not been plainly understood— like many another word of God! The man had searched and the spirit of man had been searched, with the result that Daniel set his face to seek Jehovah God, with fasting, and sackcloth and ashes (Daniel 9:4). He prayed—and made confession.

My spirit and your spirit will not see the divine logic here without the operation of the Holy Spirit upon our spirits. Those who had sinned, who, in the words above quoted, had forgotten the name of their God and had spread out their hands to a strange God, had long gone to their account, and if any man could have taken up a superior attitude then Daniel could have been that man, in the consciousness of rectitude and the favour of God. He could have spoken of their sin alone, but he does not; it is, "We have sinned " (verse 4) and we read further on in verse 20, "confessing my sin and the sin of my people Israel." We see the same spirit operating in Ezra as he was made aware of the sins of the people in mixing in marriage with the people of the lands round about. It is "our iniquities" (Ezra 9) which are so much in evidence. Again, Nehemiah 1 records how that great man confessed the sins of the children of Israel, and, moreover, associated himself with them in those sins: "which we have sinned against Thee: yea, I and my father's house have sinned." These three men use similar language regarding the results of the operation of the spirit of man: Daniel says, "To us belongeth confusion of face" (verse 8); Ezra said, "O my God, I am ashamed and blush to lift up my face to Thee, my God" (verse 6); while Nehemiah wept and mourned, fasted and prayed.

The fact is, that we cannot be exercised about sin in general without the illumination which is being shed abroad upon the circumstances and sins of others finding rays to illuminate also what we are, whether by nature or practice. This is the reason why it is rarely comely to pray for others without there being confession of sin and failure, not only by others for whom we hope to pray, but by us who are seeking to draw near to God. We have repeated, and again repeat, the desirability, if not absolute necessity, of confession as an ingredient of our prayers, and we have before us three great examples of instructed men of God, not only calling upon God, but praying. True prayer, as we pointed out in our first chapter, involves judgment, according to the derivation and meaning of the word, and we said then that in prayer there should be an active, ordered, effort of mind towards discernment of persons and circumstances. The character of a Holy God is not only to be discerned, but there is a solemn necessity to turn one's thoughts to one's own personal defects and shortcomings.

The examples of prayer which we have been studying since then must have reinforced these thoughts, and in the present examples we see the truth of what we sought to teach. Ezra acknowledges the righteousness of God (verse 15), and remembers with gratitude the grace of God, in leaving a remnant to escape, in having been given a nail in His holy place, and reviving in bondage (verse 8), while Nehemiah judges the character of God, not only as a great and terrible God (verse 5), but as one that keeps covenant and mercy with them that love Him and keep His commandments, and acknowledge His power in being able to bring back His people even from the uttermost part of heaven (verse 9). After acknowledging these things and the sins committed, Nehemiah says, in a delightfully simple way, "Now these are Thy servants ... whom Thou hast redeemed by Thy great power."

Daniel is rather more explicit, but his thoughts run on parallel lines to those of Ezra and Nehemiah. Righteousness belongs unto the LORD, and mercies and forgiveness. The great plea for blessing is not upon man's worth, but upon the worth of Jehovah. "We do not present our supplications before Thee for our righteousness, but for Thy great mercies." Finally, he entreats God upon the basis of His own sake and Name: "O LORD, hearken and do; defer not: for thine own sake, O my God, because Thy city and Thy people are called by Thy Name." Abraham pleaded with God upon the same basis of the character of God. It is given unto us to plead, not only upon this same basis, but also upon the character and worth and work of our blessed Lord Jesus Christ, even as we know that all our prayers are answered by God because of Him who stands before the Throne with the evidences of His love and compassion.

ELEVEN: THE PRAYER OF JONAH

It is fitting that our studies concerning prayer should be brought to a present conclusion in connection with that prayer which Jonah uttered while in the belly of the great fish, not only because we referred to it slightly in the first chapter, but also because it sums up in itself much of the teaching expounded in that chapter. There is no doubt that the most fervent prayer is associated with the realisation of urgent need, but we have sought to show that true prayer is much more than merely calling upon God. The prayers of an understanding man are much more instructive than those of a man knowing only that he is in trouble beyond his skill to cope with, trouble that can only be helped by the intervention of an omnipotent God.

It is evident that Jonah was an understanding man, one who could judge the character of God as well as his own character and circumstances, for we read in chapter 4:2 how that he said unto God, "I knew that Thou art a gracious God, and full of compassion, slow to anger, and plenteous in mercy." This, said he, was "my saying, when I was yet in my own country," and therefore he fled to Tarshish. It is strange indeed that God should desire to use a man who would flee "from the presence of the LORD" (1:3) rather than preach a divine message, but the vessels prepared for God's use are rather imperfect, and the hand of the Great Potter is not idle to correct and to improve that which He has fashioned. It is Elihu who tells Job and his companions, that "there is a spirit in man, and the breath of the Almighty giveth them understanding" (Job 32:8). That which was desired by the Psalmist so often in Psalm 119. and by Solomon and others in the Book of Proverbs is a precious gift from God Himself, one to be cultivated and used, not only in service manward, but in approach to God.

If, in our studies, we have learnt the value of being men and women of understanding, then we shall see it made evident in our prayers. God was not prepared to let this creature of His hands fail in His duty to do the work of the Creator. We know that God is able to raise up children to Abraham even from the stones of the desert, but He has made men and intends to use them. It would have been easier, perhaps, to have used another man rather than to "prepare" a great fish, but God's ways are to a large extent beyond us. God wanted Jonah, and in smaller degree He has an object concerning each one of us. Jonah's prayer commences by calling upon God by reason of his affliction, and he likens the belly of the fish to the belly of Sheol—even so, God heard his voice. It had taken three days to bring him to such a pass that his soul fainted within him (verse 7); whether he had looked for "natural causes" to operate or not, so as to be disgorged, we cannot say, but at last he discerned the hand of God and remembered the LORD.

There is an interesting passage in the Book of Hosea which has a connection with this, and probably Hosea, whose ministry was a few years later than Jonah's, was familiar with the story. He speaks of Ephraim (5:13) discerning his sickness, and seeking remedies in Assyria. Then, after threatening to carry them off, so that there would be none to deliver, God says, "I will go and return to My place, till they acknowledge their offence, and seek My face; in their affliction they will seek Me earnestly." How true are such words, of them, of Jonah, and maybe of us! In chapter 6 Hosea entreats the people to return, saying, "... after two days will he revive us: on the third day he will raise us up, and we shall live before Him. And let us know, let us follow on to know the LORD." In chapter 14:2, Hosea says to Israel, "Take with you words, and return unto the LORD: say unto Him, Take away all iniquity ... so will we render as bullocks the offering of our lips."

Hosea was a man of understanding also, and spoke by the Spirit of God. His words are almost a commentary on the prayer of Jonah. Apart from the reviving after two days and being raised up on the third day, a remarkable reference, we see the hiding of God's face in the sense that Jonah realised it, when he confesses that while he had fled from the presence of the LORD, it was the LORD that had cast him from before His eyes. There was a sense of loss to Jonah; true life was impossible, whether in the ship or in the fish, without it were lived as before God. In his affliction he sought God earnestly! He desired to live before God, yes, to look again toward the holy temple of God (verse 4), and his prayer thus came in unto God, into His holy temple (verse 7). Very truly had Jonah come to know the meaning of life; life without understanding is as death; an understanding man will come to know in ever-increasing measure the fullness of life, which is the knowledge of God. As Hosea so aptly put it: "And let us know, let us follow on to know the LORD."

Again in the words of Hosea, Jonah was prepared to take with him words to set before the LORD, and desired to render as bullocks the offering of his lips. Confession of iniquity is taught by Hosea and practised by Job as something desirable in prayer, but forgiveness is not all. The man who has prayed to God in an understanding way will see that there are things to render to God, even the fruit of lips that make confession to His name. Jonah was prepared to do that which was fitting: "I will sacrifice unto Thee with the voice of thanksgiving; I will pay that which I have vowed." In our first chapter, and oft-times since, we have stressed the teaching of the Scriptures on this matter of the sacrifice of thanksgiving, that which is called the cup of salvation in Psalm 116.14 (compare verses 13-14 with verses 17-18).

How delightful for the prepared vessel of God, coming fresh from the recent efforts of the Great Potter, to lift up his voice in rendering unto God the sacrifices of thanksgiving - of this it is said in Psalm 50:23: "Whoso offereth the sacrifice of thanksgiving glorifieth Me."

Did you love *Under the Old Covenant*? Then you should read *Wisdom from a Watchman* by Jack Ferguson!

The late Jack Ferguson was known for being a "watchman on the walls", always alert to present or future dangers, challenges and opportunities for those that he pastored. This collection of some of his writings typifies his gentle, yet insightful ministry that is as perceptive now as it was when it was written.

Also by DR. A.T. DOODSON

Sacrifices and Offerings Under the Old Covenant
The Festivals of Jehovah Under the Old Covenant
Lessons from Prayer Under the Old Covenant
Under the Old Covenant

About the Author

Arthur Thomas Doodson was born in Lancashire, England in 1890. Although born profoundly deaf, in his secular career he was an expert on tidal analysis and became a Fellow of the Royal Society in 1933, and was also recognized as a Commander of the British Empire. His work is best known for providing the British Army with a prediction of the best tidal and light conditions for the D-Day Landing in 1944.

However, Doodson devoted his life not to science, but to Jesus Christ, and was an elder and leader amongst the Churches of God until his death in 1968, aged 78. Doodson provided the impetus for the periodical "Young Mens Corner", which became Bible Studies in 1933 and is still published today, and was an editor and contributor for many years.

About the Publisher

Hayes Press (www.hayespress.org) is a registered charity in the United Kingdom, whose primary mission is to disseminate the Word of God, mainly through literature. It is one of the largest distributors of gospel tracts and leaflets in the United Kingdom, with over 100 titles and hundreds of thousands despatched annually. In addition to paperbacks and eBooks, Hayes Press also publishes Plus Eagles Wings, a fun and educational Bible magazine for children, and Golden Bells, a popular daily Bible reading calendar in wall or desk formats. Also available are over 100 Bibles in many different versions, shapes and sizes, Bible text posters and much more!

www.ingramcontent.com/pod-product-compliance
Lightning Source LLC
Chambersburg PA
CBHW031354040426
42444CB00005B/290